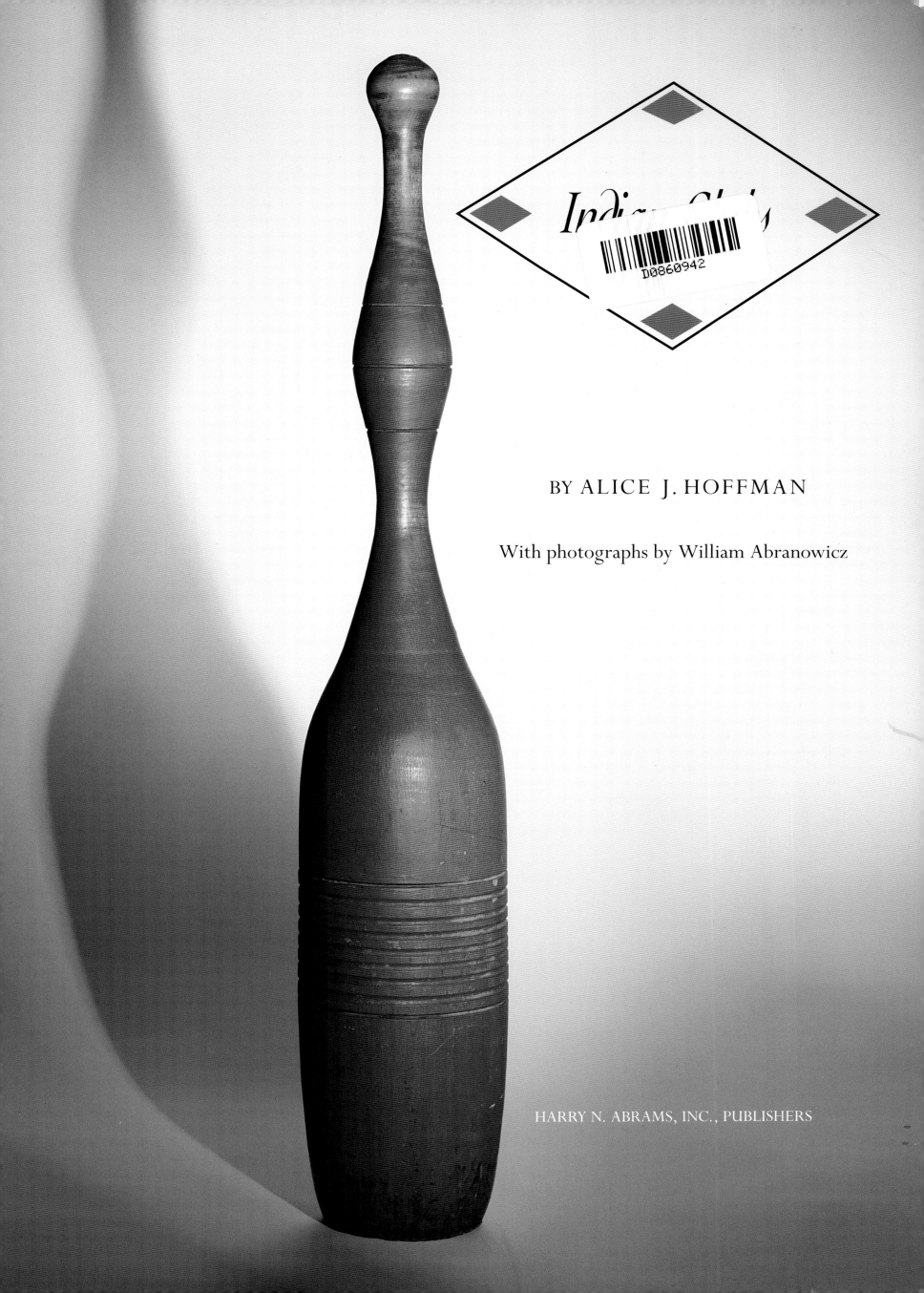

Indian Clubs

BY ALICE J. HOFFMAN

With photographs by William Abranowicz

HARRY N. ABRAMS, INC., PUBLISHERS

Dedication

To my husband Ronald, without whom this book never would have been a reality.
For over twenty-six years, he has been my guiding light and most ardent supporter.
I am thankful that he shares my passion for collecting, that he encourages me
to take risks and to seek new paths, and that he spotted that first pair of
Indian clubs with his incredible "eye." But most of all I love him
because he appreciates creativity over the perfect sentence.

To my father Jean, who loved me
and always made me feel I could do anything.
I wish he were here to share this accomplishment.

Page 1: Artist unknown. *Orange Lady*. c. 1860s–1930s.
Painted wood, H 30 x Diam. 5¼″, Weight 10 lbs. Private collection

This club is unique in form. Like a Jean Arp sculpture, the sensuous silhouette
of the club is at once feminine in nature and bold in stature,
embracing the space around it. No mate has been found for this club,
which was probably homemade on a lathe.

Editor: Elisa Urbanelli
Designer: Carol Robson

Archival material photographed
by Gavin Ashworth

Library of Congress Catalog Card Number: 96–83738
ISBN 0–8109–2670–9

Text and archival material copyright © 1996 Alice J. Hoffman
Principal photographs copyright © 1996 William Abramowicz

Published in 1996 by Harry N. Abrams, Incorporated, New York
A Times Mirror Company

Printed and bound in Hong Kong

Contents

Foreword

Knowledge about the everyday things of life is remarkably transitory. Objects stored away in closets and attics may elicit such fond memories that one is encouraged to keep them, but the personal associations of one generation rarely are transmitted to the next with the same sense of immediacy. Ultimately the things around which we organize the various aspects of our lives, along with the knowledge of how we came to acquire them, how they were used, and why we cared about them are discarded or lost. This is especially true of objects that no longer seem to serve a useful purpose.

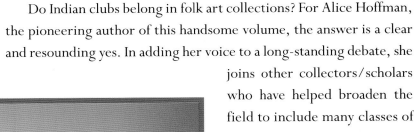

Visit any large country antique shop and you will see objects like these, once useful, once invested with meaning and memories, stacked up on shelves or gathering dust in corners. Even set out this way, devoid of context, they are often resonant of other times and places, artifacts of old ways that draw us into our own pasts. Invariably there are some objects among the others that evoke nothing so much as mystery; we may admire them for their form or workmanship or ornamentation but we only have the vaguest notions about their origins or purposes.

Although barely fifty years have passed since they were in common use, Indian clubs are clearly in this latter category, so little are they known today. To be sure, some, but not many, Americans may remember calisthenic exercises with Indian clubs early in the century, and even they must have put their clubs away long ago and forgotten them. Exercises with Indian clubs played a role in intercollegiate gymnastics into the first two or three decades of the present century, but clubs are no longer to be found lined up like wooden soldiers along the walls of gymnasiums. With the passage of time, some Indian clubs have found their way to antique shops and auctions of Americana, where often they have confused experts, and at least a few may now be seen in fine collections of American folk art.

Do Indian clubs belong in folk art collections? For Alice Hoffman, the pioneering author of this handsome volume, the answer is a clear and resounding yes. In adding her voice to a long-standing debate, she joins other collectors/scholars who have helped broaden the field to include many classes of objects not originally contemplated as works of American folk art. Indeed, prior to the advent of American folk art scholarship in the 1920s, most of these objects were understood simply as things of utility, household decoration, or personal fancy. The field has continued to expand, however, and such previously familiar things as windmill weights and fish decoys and even walking sticks, and scores of the more common objects of daily life are comfortably ensconced within its welcoming, if uncertain, boundaries.

Like some other examples of American folk sculpture, Indian clubs are utilitarian in nature, but often bear striking surface ornamentation with no purpose other than to please the eye. This is often the way that objects of utility become objects of beauty or even works of art. The illustrations in this book demonstrate not only the creativity of the gifted persons who decorated Indian clubs, but also the resourcefulness of the collectors who have found places in their homes for them.

Whether or not Alice Hoffman convinces you that Indian clubs belong in collections of American folk art, she certainly demonstrates how compelling these simple forms may be in the hands of a skillful artist. She also tells a fascinating story of a time when Americans exercised vigorously and artfully, seeking grace and strength in movement, but without the complex machinery of today's gymnasiums or health clubs. She has recovered an all but forgotten subchapter in the history of American sport and, at the same time, helped us appreciate another aspect of American artistic creativity. Hats off to her!

Gerard C. Wertkin
Director
Museum of American Folk Art

Above: The superb craftsmanship and design that characterize an elegant Shaker rocker are reflected in the Indian clubs that stand beside it. There is no documentation, however, that Shakers made or used Indian clubs.

Opposite: Artist unknown. *Indian Club "ETW 1892."* 1892. Polychromed wood, H 20 x Diam. 4 ½", Weight 1/2 lb. Collection of Roger and Alyce Rose

The design of this black and orange painted club (one of a pair) is characteristic of the Aesthetic Movement. Initialed "ETW" and dated 1892, the club features brass tacks around the neck.

Introduction
INDIAN CLUBS AS AN EXPRESSION OF AMERICAN FOLK ART

What is folk art? "Art of the common man"? Objects created within the context of a community? A social history? A personal instinctive expression? Suggesting all of these things, the term "folk art" is difficult to define.[1] It is constantly unfolding and subject to change, discovery, and challenge. Provocative debate among scholars, curators, art historians, collectors, and dealers assures that interest in folk art will continue to grow. Depending upon which point of view one adopts, or even fashions, folk art can encompass a vast spectrum of creative production, including utilitarian objects from the preindustrial period made by untrained or nonacademic artists, decorative and mass-produced objects from the industrial era, or the personal and often psychological expressions of today's outsider art. What is clear is that folk art is a field that is evolving and broadening as new material comes to light.[2]

Objects characterized today as American folk art possess both artistic merit and historical association. Many folk art objects were originally created for utilitarian purposes, and therefore they reflect aspects of a period's cultural identity. But beyond that, these objects are now considered folk art because their makers exerted a conscious effort to enhance the objects above the purely utilitarian, either by adornment or refinement.[3] In an attempt to put folk art in perspective, Holger Cahill, a curator and collector who mounted two groundbreaking exhibitions in the early 1930s, described American folk sculpture as "art of the common man."

These sculptures were made by anonymous craftsmen and amateur carvers, carpenters, cabinetmakers, shipwrights, blacksmiths, stonecutters, metal workers, sailors, farmers and laborers. The work of these men . . . is folk art in its truest sense—it is an expression of the common people and not an expression of a small cultured class. Folk art usually has not much to do with the fashionable art of its period. It is never the product of art movements, but comes out of craft traditions, plus that personal something of the rare craftsman who is an artist by nature if not by training. This art . . . goes straight to the fundamentals of art—rhythm, design, balance, proportion, which the folk artist feels instinctively.[4]

Objects considered to be folk art include gravestones, handcrafted and commercially made weathervanes, quilts, coverlets, windmill weights, doorstops, carousel horses, cigar store figures, ships' figureheads, trade signs, fire marks, boot jacks, iron stove plates, hitching posts, decoys, and chalkware figures. What seems to unify these disparate objects is a practical dimension. Even folk paintings, such as those of Ammi Phillips, Joseph H. Davis, and James Bard were originally created not solely as works of art but also as documents to record for posterity a family member and his or her possessions, residence, farm, or profession.[5]

Indian clubs, a form of exercise apparatus of the late nineteenth and early twentieth centuries, were both handcrafted and commercially produced. They are represented here for the first time as American folk art.

The clubs originated in India where they were adapted by the British Army for use in drills. Eventually, the clubs and the exercises were conveyed to England and found favor among civilians. In the 1860s, fitness enthusiast and businessman Sim. D. Kehoe introduced Indian clubs to the American market. Club swinging remained a popular form of exercise for men, women, and children in the United States through the 1930s.

The Indian club as an exercise apparatus is a social statement, an emblem marking the beginning of America's physical fitness mania. Sports clubs, gymnasiums, and school curricula of the period featured Indian club exercises, exhibitions, and contests.[6] The clubs' function, however, was not limited to developing muscle and physical prowess. Rather, many exercises were choreographed for their visual elegance and boldness of execution. In this context, the clubs were often fancifully decorated with paint or other surface treatments. The maker's ability to combine functionalism with the qualities of sculptural vigor and artistic inventiveness in the finished product is what elevates Indian clubs to the level of folk art.

Reflecting an interesting facet of the cultural life of America at the turn of the century, Indian clubs are a new "exercise" in folk art collecting. They possess a range of aesthetic qualities, from the simplicity of their intrinsic, sensuous form to their imaginative surface designs and treatments. The folk art enthusiast will appreciate Indian clubs as beautiful, sculptural objects that are not only historically intriguing but also whimsical, engaging, and visually seductive.

Indian club collecting is in its infancy. What a wonderful opportunity for a collector—new discoveries are still possible, prices are reasonable, reproductions are virtually unheard of, and, most exciting of all, there exists the chance to create a remarkable singular collection.

ORIGINS: PAST TO PRESENT

It is not the beauty or rarity of these antique objects which primarily makes their historical-record value, for indeed some of them are not intrinsically beautiful and not all of them are rare. It is their use, and so to speak, their personal histories that constitute their chief investment-for-posterity value. To this their beauty is a generous dividend.

—Scott Graham Williamson[1]

India: Myth, Symbol of Power, Physical Fitness

Indian clubs were a popular form of exercise and sport for men, women, and children in America from the 1860s through the 1930s. The Indian club can be traced to one of the most ancient weapons in India, the war club, or *gada,* a symbol of invincible physical prowess and worldly power. Almost every god and goddess of Hindu belief is depicted holding a *gada,* including Lord Vishnu, one of the principal Deities. Through the Islamic period, Rajput rulers and Muslim sultans favored the *gada* as the preferred weapon of combat. It was considered a great honor for a warrior to be trained in the use of the battle club. Through the ages, the war club changed in both name and form. Eventually, its use evolved in India as a means of physical exercise.[2]

The British: Discovery, Adaptation, Export

During the nineteenth century merchants, missionaries, travelers, and officers of the British army stationed in India gave accounts of Indian-club swinging as a recreational sport and a means of developing physical strength. An English officer noted:

> The wonderful club exercise is one of the most effectual kinds
> of athletic training, known anywhere in common use
> throughout India. The Clubs are of wood, varying in weight
> according to the strength of the person using them, and in
> length about two feet and a half, and some six or seven inches
> in diameter at the base, which is level, so as to admit of their
> standing firmly when placed on the ground, and thus
> affording great convenience for using them in the swinging
> positions. The exercise is in great repute among the native
> soldiery, police and others whose caste renders them liable to
> emergencies where great strength of muscle is desirable.
> The evolutions which the Clubs are made to perform, in
> the hands of one accustomed to their use, are exceedingly
> graceful, and they vary almost without limit. Beside the great
> recommendation of simplicity, the Indian Club practice
> possesses the essential property of expanding the chest and
> exercising every muscle in the body concurrently.[3]

Realizing the beneficial character of this type of athletic training, the British army adapted Indian-club exercises as part of its own military exercise drill. The British public subsequently embraced this new sport. A Mr. Harrison, a professor of gymnastics and considered the strongest man in England during the 1860s, developed a routine of swinging a pair of Indian clubs as a means of improving physical fitness. Queen Victoria recognized the skill and grace exhibited by Harrison and presented him with a vase as a token of her praise.[4] The Queen's approval of this new method of physical exercise provided a legitimacy to Indian-club swinging that was not lost on the English public or, for that matter, on the American public that patterned its tastes and styles after England during Queen Victoria's reign (1837–1901).[5]

America's Fascination

Sim. D. Kehoe, a well-known nineteenth-century American proponent of exercise and a manufacturer of gymnastic equipment, observed Professor Harrison demonstrate the art of Indian-club swinging during a visit to England in June 1861. Kehoe marveled at the grace and agility Harrison exhibited, certain that he had found the perfect exercise. Upon his return to America, Kehoe espoused the health and fitness benefits to be gained through club swinging. He refined the shape of the Indian club and, in 1862, began to manufacture and sell clubs to the public. Four years later Kehoe wrote *The Indian Club Exercise,* believed to be the first American publication dedicated entirely to the sport. His publisher reported:

> [Kehoe] has built up a business which is hardly yet matured
> and in the course of time will have its agencies in every
> city and town in the country. It would be utterly impossible
> to enumerate the names of well known celebrities in any
> sport who use Mr. Kehoe's Clubs . . . among them the
> celebrated crews of Harvard and Yale . . . Base-Ball
> Clubs—the Champion Atlantics, of Brooklyn, N.Y.,
> Mutuals, of New York, and Athletics, of Philadelphia. . . .
> [I]n the billiard community the Clubs are esteemed invaluable.
> . . . [I]n the severe training undergone by those who engage
> in pugilistic encounters, the Club is an indispensable adjunct
> . . . . Nor are the beneficial effects of the Club exercise by any
> means confined to professionals of the various manly sports
> and pastimes. Merchants, bankers, clerks and those engaged
> in daily business pursuits who need some available means of
> exercise to counteract the ills arising from their sedentary
> occupations, are many of them becoming experts with
> the clubs, and reaping the everlasting benefits.[6]

Ulysses S. Grant, then Lieutenant General of the United States Army, wrote to Kehoe in April 1866:

> I have the pleasure of acknowledging the receipt of a full
> set of rosewood Dumb-Bells and Indian Clubs, of your
> manufacture. They are of the nicest workmanship. Please
> accept my thanks for your thus remembering me, and
> particularly my boys, who I know will take great delight
> as well as receive benefit in using them.[7]

Societal and religious factors at work in America during the postwar period of the 1860s were instrumental in ensuring the popularity

Sim. D. Kehoe

Above: S. D. Kehoe is credited with introducing the Indian club to America. Upon his return from England in 1861, Kehoe refined the shape of the club and began to manufacture and sell clubs to the public. Etching from *The Indian Club Exercise* (1866).

Right: An unidentified African-American "pugilist," c. 1900, with a pair of large, hand-hewn clubs.

The Touch.

Lifting the weights.

Dumb Bell.

Indian Clubs.

Graeco-Roman Wrestling.

Cannon Balls.

Velocipede Race.

Above: Organized calisthenics and physical exercise were seen as liberating and as a means of achieving and preserving good health. *Harper's Weekly,* in 1860, coined the term "Athletic Revival" in describing this phenomenon. This illustration of Athletic Games at Gilmore's Concert Garden, New York, from *Harper's Weekly* (Dec. 18, 1875), depicts the role of Indian clubs in the exercise regime.

Opposite: A. G. Spalding & Bros. was one of the most popular manufacturers of Indian clubs. One of the company's advertisements from c. 1910 offers several different grades of clubs: "Gold Medal" clubs, made of selected first grade clear maple; "Model ES" clubs, made of "good material"; and "Exhibition" clubs, made for exhibition and stage purposes. The latter, finished in ebonite, were deliberately made hollow and with a large body, resembling a club weighing three pounds or more.

and acceptance of organized calisthenics and gymnastics, especially Indian-club exercises. With the onset of the Industrial Revolution, Americans were living in towns and cities in greater numbers each year, working in factories and offices rather than outdoors and on the land. The resulting sedentary lifestyle was considered a danger to one's well-being, both physically and spiritually. A routine of physical exercise was seen as liberating and as a means of achieving and preserving good health. "Muscular Christianity," a religious movement established in England during the last half of the nineteenth century and embraced by many Americans, equated morality and godliness with exercise. To be a good Christian one needed to be physically fit.

> Perfection of the body was an essential part of Christian morality in this system of thought. . . . The gymnasium became one urban gathering place where, like the church, groups of like minded people might get to know their neighbors and combat the health and moral hazards of the big city.[8]

Harper's Weekly, in 1860, coined the term "Athletic Revival" in describing this phenomenon.[9]

Kehoe's Indian clubs, "missives of Muscular Christianity,"[10] emerged as one of the most popular methods of linking spiritual health with physical vigor. Exercise enthusiasts and manufacturers of

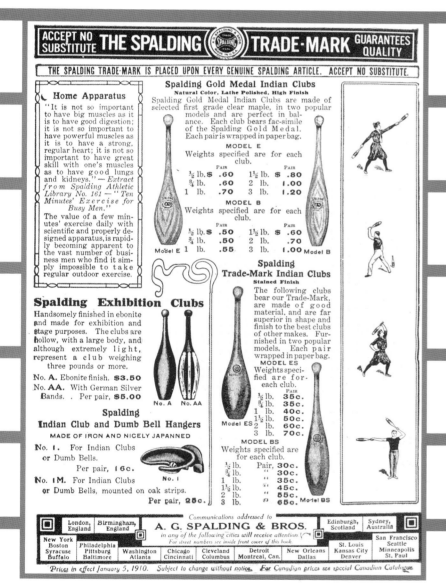

physical fitness equipment, such as Edward B. Warman of Los Angeles, J. H. Dougherty of New York, and A. G. Spalding & Bros. of New York, Chicago, Philadelphia, and Chicopee, Massachusetts, followed Kehoe's example and began to manufacture Indian clubs. Dougherty, in 1892, noted, "there is a fascination about this exercise that grows on one with proficiency. . . . The present generation is the first which had an opportunity of enjoying the exercise in this country. It will not, however, be the last."[11]

Top: A. G. Spalding & Bros. *Manufacturer's Label.* Model E. S. Stamped

Above: A. G. Spalding & Bros. *Manufacturer's Label.* Gold Medal series. Decal

Self-proclaimed "ministers" of health and exercise wrote manuals and textbooks detailing the method and endorsing Indian-club exercises. Dr. Dioclesian Lewis, an American physician and physical education instructor, advocated incorporating an exercise

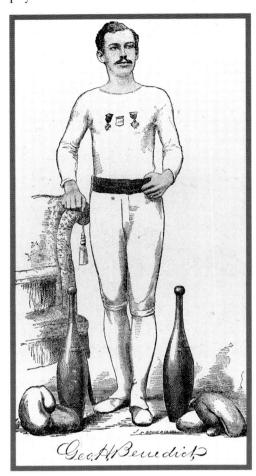

Geo. H. Benedict,

program into the daily routine of all men, women, and children. His philosophy made him one of the most widely respected leaders of the Athletic Revival movement. He believed clubs to be "indispensable to harmonious training and that no gymnasium was complete without them."[12] In the twenty-fourth edition of his book *New Gymnastics for Men, Women and Children,* published in 1888, Lewis described the ideal club: "[made] of black walnut, very smooth, kept scrupulously clean and . . . 20″ long and 4″ thick for men, 18″ long and 3″ thick for women and 15″ long and 2″ thick for small people."[13]

16 ∗ ∗ ∗ THE GYMNASIUM.

SCHOOL
Gymnastic Apparatus.
MUSICAL DUMB-BELLS

WANDS.
DUMB-BELLS.
INDIAN CLUBS.

BEST MODELS AND FINISH.

SCHOOL ROOM OUTFIT.

Four Dozen dowel Wands with Rack and Manual, net price, $1.00.
Eighty (80) of these outfits in use in one city.
Send for Circulars.

NARRAGANSETT MACHINE CO.
PROVIDENCE, R. I.

Above left: George H. Benedict, author of Wright & Ditson's *Complete Manual of Boxing, Club-Swinging & Dumbbell Exercise,* was a champion club swinger and considered "best" amateur boxer in the West in 1881.

Left: The Narragansett Machine Co., manufacturers and distributors of gymnastic equipment, published a monthly journal, *The Gymnasium.* This advertisement for "School Gymnastic Apparatus," including Indian clubs, was featured in the Sept.–Oct. 1895 issue.

Above: Championship medals, trophies, and commemorative jewelry were awarded to athletes who excelled in Indian-club exercises. Advertisements, catalogues, and manuals illustrating typical exercises can be found dating back to the 1860s. Salesmen's samples were made of wood and metal and included full size but hollow clubs as well as miniatures.

Benjamin Gardiner, in his 1884 manual *Indian Club Swinging by an Amateur,* noted:

> The exercise with the Indian Club, while excelled by none in prompt and beneficial results, is at once the least expensive and the most convenient of modern recreations. These qualities of cheapness and convenience strongly commend it to that large class in every community which lacks either the means or the leisure to indulge in more elaborate and costly diversions. The expense of the club-swinger's equipment, including a light and a heavy set of clubs, a suitable habit, and an instruction book, need not exceed the moderate sum of ten or fifteen dollars.[14]

M. Bornstein devoted separate chapters to women and children in *Manual of Instruction in the Use of Dumb Bell, Indian Club, and Other Athletic Exercises,* published in 1889. He emphasized the importance of exercise as a way to develop one's mental abilities and as a means to ensure health and strength to the whole body:

> Indian club exercises have of late years become one of the most universal methods of developing the muscular anatomy of the human body. Schools, colleges and even theological seminaries have adopted their use. . . . My experience . . . warrants me to distinctly state that there is no exercise . . . so positive in its results [as] the handling of Indian Clubs.[15]

Regarding Indian-club exercises for children, Bornstein prescribed:

> If parents would inoculate in the minds of their offspring . . . the absolute necessity of a course of muscular training . . . their hearts would be gladdened by seeing them exuberant in spirits and in glowing health and strength. However, there is one thing I desire to impress upon you . . . these exercises should not be taken from . . . play time, and nothing be introduced at play time but play.[16]

Indian-club exercises varied greatly in complexity, ranging from simple lifts to one- and two-club exercises of elaborate circles and arcs (overleaf). In an attempt to simplify these exercises, letters of the alphabet were applied to specific movements. Gardiner noted that this "greatly facilitates lucid description, furnishes a simple formula for each swing, obviates the necessity of complicated diagrams and renders self instruction practicable and comparatively easy."[17] Moreover, he suggested that exercise attire be "a loosely fitting habit of soft flannel . . . light and easy fitting, [with] suitable regard being paid also to strength and durability of fabric."[18]

Gymnasiums throughout the country held exhibitions and competitions. Schools and universities offered courses in Indian-club swinging. The March–April 1895 edition of *The Gymnasium,* a monthly publication devoted to physical education, included advertisements for summer school programs that included Indian-club instruction. Harvard and Vanderbilt Universities, the Chautauqua School of Physical Education in New Haven, Connecticut, and the Posse Gymnasium of Boston, Massachusetts, were among the advertisers. In 1908, W. G. Anderson, M.D., Professor of Physical Education and Director of Gymnasium at Yale University, noted in his introduction to *Club Swinging for Physical Exercise and Recreation*: "That the Indian Club is the only piece of light apparatus adopted by the collegiate and intercollegiate gymnastic societies is an argument in its favor not to be lightly passed by."[19] The

Above: These young women look none too happy. Perhaps their instructor failed to heed J. Watson's advice that "harsh treatment must be carefully avoided, much more than anything like turning the student's involuntary awkwardness or his first failures, into ridicule. He must never forget . . . the pleasure of the various exercises." The young women are Turners (German-American exercise enthusiasts), shown with their instructor and Indian clubs, c. 1900.

Below: This turn-of-the-century photograph depicts a grade school exercise class in Long Island City, New York. According to M. Bornstein's *Manual of Instruction in the Use of Dumb Bell, Indian Club, and Other Athletic Exercises* (1889), "Schools, colleges, and even theological seminaries have adopted [Indian clubs] in their respective institutions with the most beneficial results. For keeping the body in a healthy and vigorous condition there has as yet been nothing invented which for its simplicity and gracefulness can be favorably compared with the Indian Club exercise."

"And now a word to the ladies. Exercise for woman is as essential as it is for man. It is an indisputable fact that a system of light exercise gives precision and action to the muscles, it will not only give strength but add greatly to the natural gracefulness in women; and if with a light pair of Clubs . . . they would go through a routine of exercise for fifteen minutes in the morning and at night before retiring, they would greatly enhance their bodily strength; and after practicing for a few months, their chests will begin to expand and their arms become plump and muscular. And what lady would not be proud of a well developed form, a beautifully shaped arm, a high chest and an erect carriage?" From M. Bornstein, *Manual of Instruction in the Use of Dumb Bell, Indian Club, and Other Athletic Exercises* (1889). Engraving from Sim. D. Kehoe, *The Indian Club Exercise* (1866).

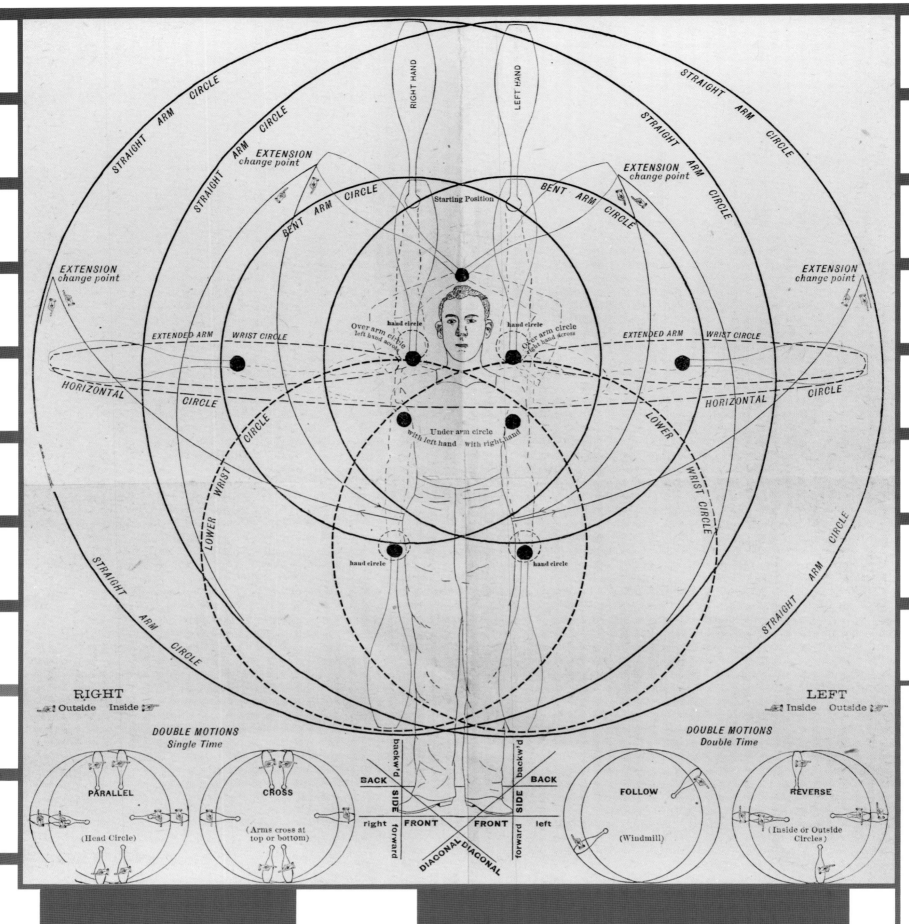

The illustration contains the following labels:

RIGHT HAND · LEFT HAND

STRAIGHT ARM CIRCLE · STRAIGHT ARM CIRCLE · STRAIGHT ARM CIRCLE · STRAIGHT ARM CIRCLE

EXTENSION change point · EXTENSION change point

BENT ARM CIRCLE · BENT ARM CIRCLE

Starting Position

EXTENSION change point · EXTENSION change point

EXTENDED ARM · WRIST CIRCLE · WRIST CIRCLE · EXTENDED ARM

hand circle · hand circle

Over arm circle left hand across · Over arm circle right hand across

HORIZONTAL CIRCLE · HORIZONTAL CIRCLE

LOWER WRIST CIRCLE · LOWER WRIST CIRCLE

Under arm circle with left hand · with right hand

hand circle · hand circle

STRAIGHT ARM CIRCLE · STRAIGHT ARM CIRCLE

RIGHT — Outside   Inside · LEFT — Inside   Outside

DOUBLE MOTIONS Single Time · DOUBLE MOTIONS Double Time

PARALLEL (Head Circle) · CROSS (Arms cross at top or bottom) · FOLLOW (Windmill) · REVERSE (Inside or Outside Circles)

BACK · SIDE · backw'd · backw'd · SIDE · BACK
right forward · FRONT · FRONT · forward left
DIAGONAL · DIAGONAL

Above: *Wright & Ditson's Complete Manual of Boxing, Club-Swinging & Dumb Bell Exercise* (c. 1880s) included this illustration of one of the more complex exercises.

Opposite, clockwise from top left:

S. D. Kehoe's *The Indian Club Exercise* provided diagrams for club swingers to follow. Here, a simple lift, Exercise No. 2: "Carry the Clubs to the position shown in the figure, and then raise and lower them slowly, as shown by the dotted lines. Keep both Clubs in a horizontal position, and parallel to the floor line. Repeat slowly until fatigued."

A bimanual exercise of circles and arcs, Exercise No. 13: "This exercise is more difficult to describe than to execute. It is familiarly known as the 'Windmill,' from its resemblance to the four arms of a windmill following each other round and round, in one direction."

A one-club exercise, Exercise No. 9: "You may take as heavy a one as you can use, or about double the weight of those used in pairs—say from ten to twenty pounds."

Kehoe also used letters of the alphabet to simplify specific exercises. Exercise No. 7: "'The Moulinet' . . . It will be found, by a little practice, that the movement is not at all difficult, but depends on relaxing the grasp and throwing in the elbows at the proper time, that the circle may be described fairly and squarely, as indicated in the figure."

Left: A properly outfitted young woman demonstrates the use of Indian clubs in this c. 1895 photograph. According to Dio Lewis's *New Gymnastics* (1888), "In the ladies' costume, perfect liberty about the waist and shoulders is the desideratum. . . . The belt should be several inches longer than the waist, and the dress about the shoulders very loose. . . . The stockings should, for cold weather, be thick woollen . . . ; the shoes, strong with broad soles and low heels."

Right: Brass shirt studs in the shape of Indian clubs were one of many jewelry designs available for club enthusiasts.

American College of Physical Education, in Chicago, Illinois, offered elementary and advanced courses in Indian-club exercises as late as 1916. The "Indian Club Race," a competition first held in 1864, was still in use by the Department of the Interior, Bureau of Education, in 1927.[20]

Indian-club exercises became so popular that enthusiasts could purchase commemorative jewelry, often in the shape of clubs. Kehoe himself, in 1866, is known to have presented J. Edward Russell, an amateur athlete from New York City, with a gold medal designed and manufactured by the Tiffany Company of New York.[21]

Despite Dougherty's proclamation of 1892, that "the Indian Club, unlike many equally modern innovations, [has] come to stay,"[22] by the 1930s Indian-club exercises had become the object of ridicule and their popularity began to wane. The Roaring '20s signaled the demise of Victorian mores, as new freedoms came to overshadow the religious fervor and social constraints of the past. America's fascination with and moral attachment to physical fitness gave way to speakeasies, dance halls, and a more carefree lifestyle. The publication *BallyHoo* featured a full-page parody in 1933, "Indian Club Mania Grows," mocking the use of Indian clubs as the foolish practice of fanatics.[23] A. G. Spalding & Bros., one of the last companies to manufacture clubs, discontinued their production in the 1930s.[24]

While America's obsession with physical fitness has undergone a resurgence since the 1970s, Indian clubs are now valued as objects of folk art rather than as a instruments of maintaining one's physical and spiritual well-being. They are remarkable for their sculptural simplicity, artistic strength, and inventive, expressive character.

INDIAN CLUB MANIA GROWS

Two new cases develop daily and quarantine is threatened. Vile craze eating at very moral fibre of society.

BALLYHOO doesn't mind a little fooling, but this is going too doddam far. Just look at these actual photographs snapped by a staff photographer at McCloskey's Turnverein.

Left: Despite J. H. Dougherty's proclamation of 1892 that "the Indian Club, unlike many equally modern innovations, [has] come to stay," by the 1930s Indian club exercises had become the object of ridicule. The magazine *BallyHoo* featured a full-page parody, "Indian Club Mania Grows," in its Feb. 1933 issue.

An addict executing "The Bungstarter Swipe," one of the ugly movements of this nefarious practice. Can be had in peach, beige or mamoreuse. Now we ask you.

While built wholly on an axiom—and having quite a can—this gent is the first to solve the Pythagorean Theorem with both clubs behind his back. Certainly a dirty trick, at best.

Here we see Mr. Kleinert designing dress shields. Mrs. Kleinert, in rear, is about to tap the mister smartly on the conk. Poor Mr. Kleinert.

Our subject has just seen a cockeyed gymnast and has his clubs crossed. Or maybe he's fighting off hornets.

Not alone confined to the menfolk, mind you, here we see one of the "Fairer Sex" mumbling, "Just wait till I lay my hands on that flat-face husband of mine." Madame is brushing up on the "hang-one-on-you" stroke. Is nothing held sacred?

A pretty pass, indeed. Here a mother is seen lighting the children to bed . . . and with her pants hanging down that way, too.

This fellow lost his shirt in the market and is going around in circles. Can this go on?

Mrs. Culberson announces an opening two club bid, one up and one down. Why, it's getting so one Indian doesn't know what the other one's doing.

Opposite: The number "12" on the uniforms of the teenage girls in this c. 1890 photograph suggests that this was a competitive team.

Right: The masthead for the Narragansett Machine Co.'s monthly publication *The Gymnasium* featured a rack of wall-mounted Indian clubs and dumbbells.

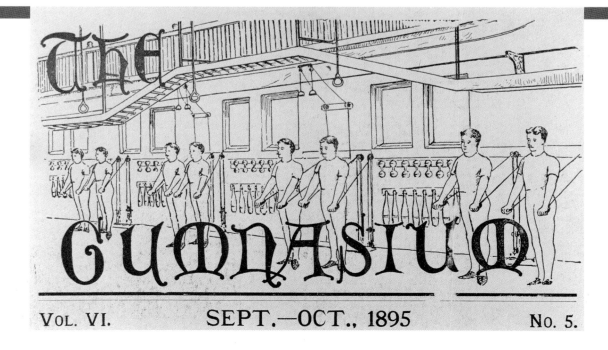

THE GYMNASIUM

VOL. VI.   SEPT.—OCT., 1895   NO. 5.

Chapter Two

COLLECTING INDIAN CLUBS

The works embraced by the term "folk art"—paintings, sculpture, and utilitarian objects—are incredibly diverse. Although to an extent these types must be evaluated using different guidelines, there are fundamental criteria that apply to all: authenticity, condition, quality of design, and attribution.

—*Robert Bishop and Judith Reiter Weissman*[1]

How does one go about collecting Indian clubs? The first challenge is to become as knowledgeable as possible about the history and production of these objects. Yet, Indian club collecting is in its infancy, and there is much still to learn. Dealers, collectors, and museums have not had an opportunity to determine if there exists commonality or consistency in such elements as design, material, construction, or historical detail. The good news is that, as a result, there is not presently a financial incentive for reproduction. As Indian clubs become more widely known and collected, however, it is likely they too will enter the not-so-exclusive club of reproductions. Nonetheless, forming an Indian club collection according to specific guidelines—shape, size, weight, manufacturer, and surface treatment—will allow the collector to establish authenticity, quality of design, and proper attribution, essential criteria in the evaluation of all folk art.

Shape, Size, and Weight

Manufactured Indian clubs were turned on a lathe and produced in matching pairs. Their basic form is illustrated below. Makers individualized their Indian clubs by varying the club's shape. This led to the creation of clubs with elongated necks, fanciful turnings, and "plump" clubs with wide bases. Some clubs appear to be of Shaker origin (page 4), although there is no documentation that Shakers ever made or used Indian clubs.[2] Handmade clubs can be very irregular in form and surface (page 21), some seemingly unpaired.

Indian clubs manufactured in the United States have flat bases and can stand independently. English clubs were often rounded on the base, necessitating a rack for storage. Storage and safety concerns in gymnasiums led to the use of racks in the United States as well.

Indian clubs vary in size. Many advocates of the sport differentiated between "long clubs" and "short clubs" (pages 22–3). J. Madison Watson noted in 1864:

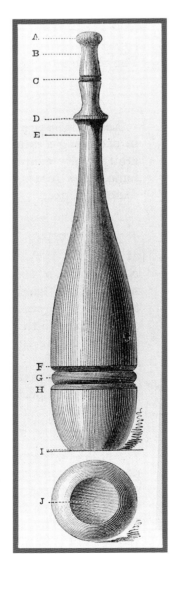

Long clubs are pleasanter to handle, and more effective in executing a number of movements, than short ones. They are specially adapted to exercise in gymnasiums, calisthenic halls, large rooms, and the open air, where there is an abundance of space.

Short clubs are more convenient, and will be found more generally useful than long ones, especially in schools and families. All of the long-club exercises may easily be executed with short clubs, while many of the short-club exercises will be found quite difficult at first, if executed with long clubs.[3]

Indeed, it was Watson who suggested that:

The length of the club [be] determined by the length of the arm. The long club, when held upon the arm extended horizontally, should reach to the point of the shoulder where the arm and shoulder join. . . . The short club in the same position should extend nearly two inches above the elbow.[4]

S. D. Kehoe, on the other hand, favored the use of long clubs:

The Indian Club exercise, as practiced at the present day in the different Gymnasiums and institutions of physical training throughout the country, is properly divided into two distinct kinds: one with the short and light Club, or Bat, and the other with the long Club, or Indian Club proper. The author does not deem it necessary to introduce the exercises for the light Club in this work, as they are only adapted for invalids and children.[5]

Indian clubs also varied in weight. As with today's barbells, athletes of varying strength and ability used clubs of different weights. Kehoe advised establishing the ideal weight by:

holding a pair [of clubs] horizontally at the side, at arm's length, letting them down to a perpendicular, and raising them again, several times, grasping them at the extremity of the handles. If this cannot be done after several trials, the Club is too heavy, and a lighter pair must be tried.[6]

The desired weight of a club was usually a function of the type of wood used in its manufacture. Ordinary clubs were made of maple or hardwoods of similar density. Light clubs were made of whitewood or ash. Heavy clubs were made of ironwood, locust, mahogany, or lignum vitae. Although Watson cautioned that "the desired weight should not be secured by varying the size,"[7] the length of a club could be used to create a fulcrum effect. A twenty-four-inch club weighing five pounds is more difficult to lift at arm's length then a twelve-inch club weighing five pounds. One manufactured club, patent stamped "March 2 '97" (page 24), had an extendible arm to vary the length and fulcrum effect. Weight could also be altered by the use of metal inserts. The hollow-base club shown on page 25 accepted interchangeable cast-iron cylinders of different weights.

The Indian clubs used most commonly for daily exercise and swinging were twelve inches in length and one-half pound in weight for children, eighteen inches in length and one and one-half pounds for women, and twenty inches in length and two and one-half to five

Right: Artist unknown. *Show Club.* c. 1875. Painted to simulate mahogany wood, H 24 x Diam. 4½″, Weight 4½ lbs.

It is unlikely that this fancifully turned single club was ever used for exercise, as the handle would be difficult and uncomfortable to grasp. The figural elements of the "neck" suggest that the craftsman was a furniture maker.

Opposite: An illustration from J. Madison Watson's *Hand-Book of Calisthenics and Gymnastics: A Complete Drill-Book for Schools Families, and Gymnasiums, with Music to Accompany the Exercises* (1864), shows the basic shape of an Indian club. Clubs manufactured in America had a flat base and could stand independently. Plain clubs did not have decorative turnings, as shown at C, D, and G of this diagram.

Above: A. G. Spalding & Bros. *Rack.* c. 1880–1903. Iron hooks mounted on oak strip, L 8′ x W 4″. Private collection

This rack of Indian clubs and dumbbells comes from an Atlantic City, New Jersey, school gymnasium. Racks were used in America for safety and economy of space. As Albert B. Wegener warned in *Graded Calisthenics and Dumb Bell Drills* (1904): "It is necessary to have Indian Club . . . hangers in order to keep the Indian Clubs . . . in proper shape. They should not be scattered around the room, but by simply putting up a pair of hangers they can be kept in good condition, and out of the way when not in use."

Opposite: Artist unknown. *Indian Club.* c. 1860s–1930s. Polychromed wood, H 30 x Diam. 5½″, Weight 5½ lbs. Private collection

One of a pair of handmade Indian clubs, painted green with white stripes, this example features an irregular surface, chisel marks, and a cracked "knot" in the wood.

Above: Artist unknown. *"Short" Indian Clubs*. c. 1860s–1930s. Polychromed wood, H 14 x Diam. 3½″, Weight ½ lb. Private collection

"Short" clubs, fourteen inches in height, are sized for women and children. The wear on the handles suggests that these clubs were used frequently.

Opposite: Artist unknown. *"Long" Indian Clubs*. c. 1860s–1930s. Polychromed wood, H 28 x Diam. 3½″, Weight ½ lb. Private collection

At twenty-eight inches in height, these "long" Indian clubs are painted black and embellished with a gold design.

Above: The design of Indian clubs sometimes allowed for adjustable weight. This pair, patent stamped "March 2, '97," features an extendible arm to vary the length and fulcrum effect.

Opposite: The lower portion of one club is detached to reveal a hollowed central core which accepts circular metal disks that alter the weight of the club.

Opposite: Artist unknown. *Circus Club, "100 LBS."* c. 1880s–1930s. Polychromed canvas and wood with tin appliqués, H 29 x Diam. 14 ", Weight 10 lbs. Private collection

Indian clubs were usually of proportionate size and weight. Despite its hefty label, this oversized club, made of canvas and wood, was a circus prop weighing a mere ten pounds.

pounds for men. Heavier weights, weighing as much as fifty pounds, were used in competitions and demonstrations.[8] Often a club's weight was stamped into the wood.

A discrepancy between size and weight might cause one to question whether an object is an Indian club. Some clubs, however, were intentionally made light and purposefully mislabeled to read 10, 20, 30 even 100 pounds. These clubs were used for demonstration purposes by salesmen and instructors, by circus performers, or by unscrupulous showmen trying to dupe the public into thinking them "Herculean."[9]

Right: Gus. Hill, "Champion Club Swinger of the World," is pictured in this 9½ x 19½" poster. Beside him is a circus club of "Herculean" size and weight. Medals, trophies, and commemorative belts, as shown, were often awarded in recognition of excellence with Indian clubs.

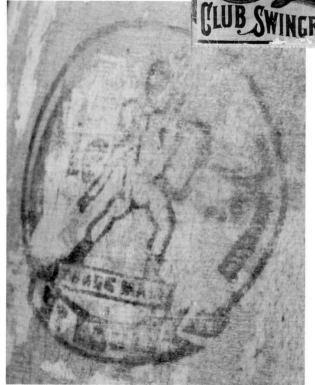

Manufacturer / Maker

An artist's signature or a firm attribution to a maker increases the value of an object. Commercially manufactured Indian clubs usually bore the label of the maker. These labels were either stamped into the wood or applied as decals. Known manufacturers include:

> The American News Company, New York
> James W. Brine Co., College Outfitters, Athletic Supplies, Cambridge, Massachusetts
> Concord Bicycle Co., Concord, New Hampshire
> D & M (The Draper & Maynard Co.), Plymouth, New Hampshire
> J. H. Dougherty, New York
> S. D. Kehoe, New York
> V. Kent (location unknown)
> Narragansett Machine Co., Providence, Rhode Island
> Horace Partridge Co., Boston, Massachusetts
> Victor Overan Wheel Co. (location unknown)
> Peck & Snyder, New York
> A. G. Spalding & Bros., New York, Chicago, Philadelphia, and Chicopee, Massachusetts
> Edward B. Warman, Los Angeles, California
> Wood & Chester (W. F. Chester), Boston, Massachusetts
> Wright & Ditson, Boston, Massachusetts

Many collectors seek a representative club of each known maker to endow their collection with historical merit. Rare labels such as Concord Bicycle are more valuable than common ones, such as A. G. Spalding & Bros. Some of the labels are themselves decorative and collectible.

Above: V. Kent. *Manufacturer's Label.* Decal

Left: *Manufacturer's Label.* Stamped

Left: Wright & Ditson. *Manufacturer's Label.* Applied

Opposite: The Draper & Maynard Co.,
Plymouth, New Hampshire.
Manufacturer's Label. D & M. Stamped

Right: James W. Brine Co., College
Outfitters, Cambridge, Massachusetts.
Manufacturer's Label. Athletic supplies. Decal

Left: Eagle with American flag.
Manufacturer's Label. Gold Coin model.
Decal

Surface Treatment

Once authenticity has been established, condition and design become deciding elements in determining a club's value. Manufactured clubs as well as handmade clubs were often embellished by their owners. This personalized treatment not only enhanced the clubs' artistic character but also served a purpose, since many Indian-club exercises were choreographed as much for their visual appeal as for their physical fitness value. As Kehoe noted: "Many of the exercises can be executed with such skill and grace as to approach 'the poetry of motion,' and when accompanied by music they can be rendered pleasing accomplishments."[10]

Period photographs, advertisements, and manuals attest to the diversity and ingenuity of decorated Indian clubs. Clubs were often painted with images of flowers, scenes, or decorative elements adapted from popular print sources of the period. Identification of the source of a design aids in dating and authenticating a club. For example, the pair of clubs on page 33 are painted with mirror views of

Right: Tom Burrows, author of *The Textbook of Club Swinging* (1910), is pictured demonstrating the use of "heavy" clubs (ten to twenty pounds). "At Cairo in September 1895 he won a trophy . . . by swinging for 26 hours 15 minutes without a stop. . . . Journeying to Montreal, Canada, he swung a pair of four pound Clubs for 43 hours 6 minutes averaging 120 swings a minute, making altogether 420,330 full circles containing 180 distinct combinations."

Below: Victor Overan Wheel Co. *Manufacturer's Label.* Decal

the Hudson Valley, echoing the nineteenth-century landscape paintings of the Hudson River School. The clubs pictured on page 32 are decorated with "Naughty Nellies," one of the more popular erotic design motifs of the late Victorian period. The Aesthetic Movement design adorning the club on page 5 dates this club to the 1890s. Other types of surface treatment include clubs encrusted with buttons (page 46), wrapped in cord (page 34), studded with fanciful furniture tacks (page 35), and personalized with initials and dates (page 37).

Kits available from manufacturers allowed owners to decorate clubs to their own taste, while lowering the cost. The Narragansett Machine Co., in 1895, offered a choice: "Either . . . the material for making the ornaments with designs, or cut ornaments will be provided if desired, so that anyone wanting a pair of ornamented clubs can get them for almost any price by doing as much of the work as he feels disposed to."[11] In addition to kits, Narragansett offered its customers three choices of "Fancy" Indian clubs with ornaments cut from thin brass which had been nickeled or plated with a gold or bronze color (pages 38–9).[12] Narragansett touted these clubs as very

Above: A group of c. 1900 Indian clubs featuring German silver appliqués and painted designs. Note the adjustable-weight club open on the floor, exposing its inner workings.

Opposite: Artist unknown. *Indian Clubs.* c. 1860s–1930s. Polychromed wood, H 22 x Diam. 5″, Weight 3½ lbs. Collection of Roger and Alyce Rose

Decoratively painted clubs, one with roses in full bloom, the other with vines and buds.

showy and especially effective, claiming, "it is the reflection from the ornaments that is the attraction of this style of club swinging."[13] Horace Partridge Exhibition Clubs could be purchased plain or with a selection of German silver or burnished copper bands in a variety of designs.

Clubs were made of different types of wood such as black and white walnut, maple, whitewood, mahogany, and rosewood. English clubs were made from willow and elm wood.[14] Each of these woods imparts a distinctive surface grain. As with furniture of the period, clubs were often painted with faux grains (pages 40–1). Other clubs were made of inlaid woods, creating intrinsic patterns (page 47).

Signs of age and wear are desirable to the collector, as long as they do not detract from a club's overall appearance, because they are evidence of use and help to recall that the club's original purpose was not ornamental. A painted surface will acquire a patina, a look of age. There should be greater wear and loss of surface finish around the neck of a club where it was held during exercise. Walnut ages to a hue of orange brown while maple becomes a golden honey color. Over the years, evaporation of the paint's natural oils will cause the paint to appear cracked or crazed and brittle. Colors, once bright and vivid, will appear subdued and darkened. Tin and copper decorative elements should be discolored, oxidized, and, if painted, show crazing. Plain wooden clubs may reveal the effects of dehydration, with cracks and discoloration. Warping is rare with turned wooden objects of thick diameter. If a piece is being added to a collection for its rarity or historical significance, surface condition may be less important.

A pair of plain Indian clubs with no other distinguishing feature can still be bought for less than sixty dollars. Clubs that exhibit good design, paint, shape, size, or weight sell for hundreds of dollars. Unique clubs, such as those bearing painted landscapes, or an inlaid set with custom carrying case (page 50) are valued in the thousands of dollars.

Above: Artist unknown. *A Floral Bouquet.* c. 1860s–1930s. Polychromed wood, H 19 x Diam. 4½″, Weight 3½ lbs. Private collection

Nineteenth-century cultural training, particularly for women, emphasized the art of drawing and painting flowers. Sources for these images were often horticultural prints, catalogues, and seed packets of the period. The artist who customized these commercially made clubs may have relied upon such sources for inspiration. Here, the floral bouquet is artfully harmonized with the contour of the clubs. The stripes and triangular designs on the base of these clubs create a bold and personal design.

Above: Artist unknown. *Naughty Nellies.* c. 19th century. Polychromed wood, H 27 x Diam. 5¼", Weight 7½ lbs. Private collection

The strict mores of the Victorian period, which promulgated the concept of women as pure and noble creatures dedicated to the home and family life, were challenged by the dramatic social changes brought on by the rise of industrialization and urbanization. In contrast to the era's puritanical image of women in society, the genre of erotic art celebrated sexual awareness. Naked ladies known as "Naughty Nellies" were among the more popular erotic design motifs. The full-bodied painted ladies on this pair of Indian clubs complement the feminine contours of the clubs themselves.

Opposite: Artist unknown. *Hudson River.* c. 1895–1910. Polychromed wood, H 18 x Diam. 4½", Weight 2½ lbs. Private collection

During the Victorian period in America, a group of artists emerged who painted landscapes with an idyllic vision of "America the Beautiful." They were collectively known as the Hudson River School after the dramatic river valley they helped immortalize. This pair of clubs displays an homage to that aesthetic. The landscape scene is further enhanced through the artist's use of Art Nouveau, Aesthetic Movement, and Japanese-inspired motifs, including sinuous, elongated forms, stylized flowers, leaves, and a peacock's tail.

Below: Artist unknown. *Cord Club.* c. 1860s–1930s. Wood with applied cord and metal tacks, H 26 x Diam. 7″, Weight 5 lbs. Private collection

One of a pair of remarkable cord-wrapped clubs. Note the use of decorative brass tacks.

Opposite: Artist unknown. *A Full Deck.* c. 1860s–1930s. Wood with applied metal design, H 20 x Diam. 4″, Weight 4 lbs. Private collection

Brass furniture tacks are used to decorate this otherwise mass-produced pair of wooden clubs. The center band features the four suits of a typical "full deck," suggesting that the owner of these clubs might have enjoyed playing cards.

Above: Peck & Snyder advertised clubs in rosewood for "Ladies' Use." The "club and biceps" featured in this 1866 advertisement was a popular image used by many late-nineteenth-century manufacturers in their manuals and advertisements.

Opposite: Artists unknown. *Indian "Initial" Clubs.* c. 1860s–1930s. Large pair, polychromed wood, H 24 x Diam. 4½″, Weight 6½ lbs.; small pair, polychromed wood with painted tin star appliqué, H 20½ x Diam. 4½″, Weight 1½ lbs. Private collection

Two pairs of manufactured Indian clubs that have been personalized with initials. The larger clubs in the foreground feature the letters "FJ" bordered by draped American flags. The smaller clubs, decorated with applied tin stars and sandpaper circles, are labeled "M. L. MG."

Opposite: Artist unknown. *Copper Flame*. c. 1860s–1930s. Polychromed wood, H 16 x Diam. 3″, Weight 1½ lbs. Private collection

Indian clubs were sold with copper and tin decoration or with appliqué kits that could be assembled by the user. This pair of clubs features an unusual stylized copper appliqué.

1077.　　1078.　　1079.

Fancy Clubs.

These Clubs are made in three weights and two styles.

Solid, Weight, 32 oz.　Price $1.20
Bored,   "　　24 oz.　　"　　1.50
Hollow, "　　12 oz.　　"　　1.80

The above are PLAIN BLACK for ornamenting. Natural Finish with wide Black Band, sound pieces. Size, 18 in. long, 4 in. diameter, would weigh 3 lbs., if made of maple.

Ornamenting $2.25, $3.00, $3.75, extra over above prices.

ALL PRICS NET.

NARRAGANSETT MACHINE CO.
PROVIDENCE, - R. I.

Above: This advertisement for "Fancy Clubs" appeared in *The Gymnasium* (Mar.–Apr. 1895). "The ornaments are cut from thin brass which has been nickeled or plated a gold or bronze color, and tacked onto the clubs with escutcheon pins. . . . This ornamentation is very durable and can be easily kept bright by polishing which is necessary, as it is the reflection from the ornaments that is the attraction of this style of club swinging."

Artists unknown. *Grain-Painted Indian Clubs.* c. 1860s–1930s. (left to right): Grain-painted to simulate mahogany, H 21 x Diam. 4½″, Weight 2½ lbs.; Grain-painted to simulate mahogany, H 16 x Diam. 2½″, Weight ½ lb.; Grain-painted to simulate rosewood, H 22½ x Diam. 4″, Weight 2½ lbs.; Grain-painted to simulate mahogany, H 16 x Diam. 2½″, Weight ½ lb. Private collection

Decorative painting was one of the most popular forms of ornamentation in the eighteenth and nineteenth centuries. Painters used one of three techniques: graining, freehand painting, and stenciling. These clubs were grain-painted to simulate expensive woods.

Below: Artist unknown. *Indian Clubs*. c. 1860s–1930s. Maple, H 17 x Diam. 2½″, Weight 1½ lbs. Private collection

The maker of this pair of clubs achieved a simplicity and strength of design that required no further embellishment. The stylized handle with its pointed tip is very unusual.

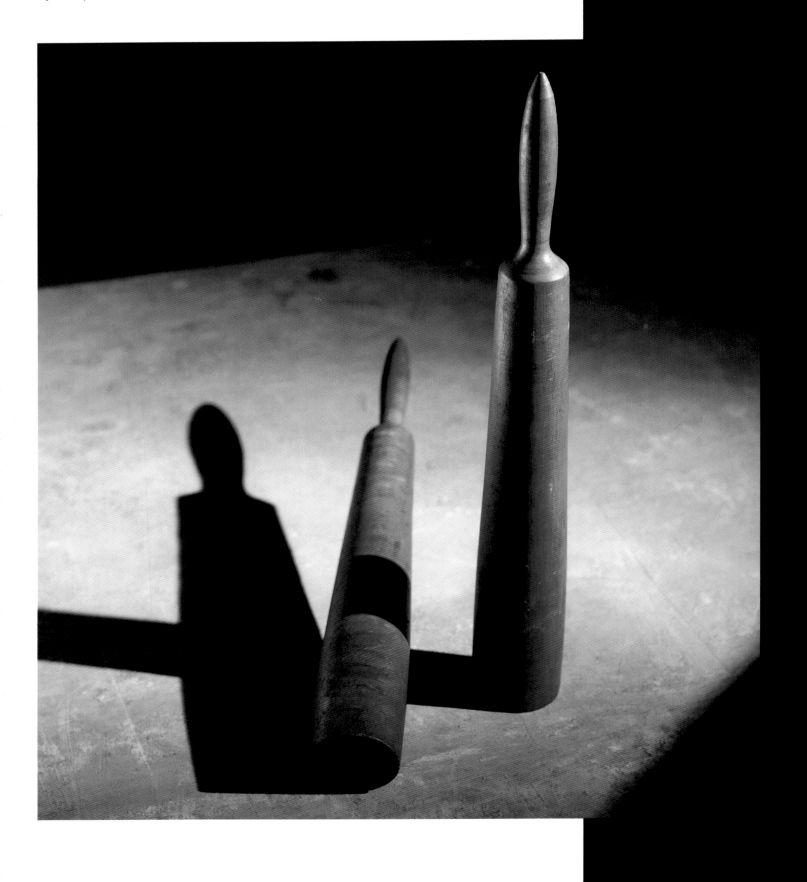

Opposite: Artist unknown. *Native American*. c. 1860s–1930s. Painted wood, H 23 x Diam. 3½″, Weight 2½ lbs. Private collection

This pair of manufactured Indian clubs painted with a striking "Native-American" design could be said to perpetuate one widely held misconception about the origin of Indian clubs.

Where to Find Indian Clubs

Where does one look for Indian clubs? Today's fascination with health and fitness is not a recent phenomenon. During the late nineteenth century it was said that "no home or gymnasium is properly furnished or complete without at least a pair [of Indian clubs]."[15] As a result, Indian clubs appear for sale throughout the United States. Most collectors find that antique shows, flea markets, and antique dealers are the best sources (see "Resource Directory," page 60). Occasionally, Indian clubs have been featured in country and city auctions. A pair of painted and gilded, turned maple Indian clubs, inscribed "G. T. Lyons," from the American folk art collection of Howard and Catherine Feldman, was featured in a 1988 auction held at Sotheby's in New York City.[16]

Above: The misconception that Indian clubs are bowling (ten) pins was unwittingly conveyed by Peck & Snyder's turn-of-the-century catalogue, *Price List of Out & Indoor Sports & Pastimes*. This advertisement for Ten Pin Balls and Pins for Bowling Alleys, features a man holding a "Kehoe" Indian club over his shoulder. Bowling pins of this period were uniform in length (18″) and weight (3 lbs., 5 oz.), bottle-shaped, and solid maple. Indian clubs varied in each of these categories and often came in woods other than maple.

" They led me bound along the winding flood,
Far in the gloomy bosom of the wood."

Misconceptions

There are several commonly held misconceptions regarding Indian clubs. To illustrate one frequent error of misidentification, there is the story of a single painted club from the American folk art collection of Mr. and Mrs. G. William Holland that sold at Sotheby's in 1995 for seven hundred and fifty dollars. The auction catalogue described this club as "an Unusual Carved and Painted Pine Bowling Pin, American, late 19th Century."[17] Bowling pins of this period were uniformly solid maple, thick-necked, bottle-shaped, eighteen inches in length, and weighed three pounds, five ounces.[18] The club from the Holland estate is hollow maple with a metal insert, seventeen and three-quarter inches in length, and weighs one and one-half pounds. The spirited bidding that took place during the auction for this club suggests that the bidders knew the true attribution of the object. It should be noted, however, that the confusion between Indian clubs and bowling pins was apparent even in the era when clubs were popular. The error was unwittingly conveyed by Peck & Snyder in its turn-of-the-century catalogue, *Price List of Out & Indoor Sports & Pastimes*. An advertisement for "Ten Pin Balls and Pins for Bowling Alleys" features an illustration of "a complete bowling alley,"[19] yet a man depicted in the illustration is holding an Indian club.

Many collectors and dealers are mistakenly of the opinion that Indian clubs are of Native-American origin. This misconception was given credence by some exercise manuals of the period. Benjamin Gardiner, for example, in his popular 1884 text *Indian Club Swinging by an Amateur*, featured Native Americans engaged in a war dance, swinging "Indian Clubs."

Finally, Indian clubs are often confused with jugglers' pins. This is not completely erroneous. As noted by Kit Summers in *Juggling with Finesse: The Definitive Book of Juggling*:

> Wooden Indian clubs . . . were . . . the first clubs used for juggling. . . . During rest period, the club swinger would play around with 1 or 2 clubs for diversion. It was only natural that eventually some pretty clever moves developed . . . and the juggling of clubs was born.[20]

Indeed, one turn-of-the-century manual entitled *Indian Club Swinging: One, Two and Three Club Juggling* provided photographs and instructions in the use of Indian clubs for juggling.[21] As juggling became more popular, clubs were made specifically for that purpose. Such "jugglers' pins" were often made of materials other than wood, such as tin and canvas. Indian clubs, on the other hand, were always made of wood.

Left: The common misconception that Indian clubs originated with Native Americans may have its source in Benjamin Gardiner's 1884 book *Indian Club Swinging by an Amateur*, which features this misleading illustration of Native Americans engaged in a war dance, swinging clubs.

"Buyer Beware"

Many popular folk art forms such as paintings, weathervanes, decoys, scrimshaw, doorstops, and furniture have been copied or altered. The most prestigious of collectors, dealers, and museums have been fooled into acquiring fakes and forgeries for their collections.[22] As the time-tested adage implores, "buyer beware." A collector must do his or her homework. There is no substitute for the knowledge of cultural and historical attributes, how an object was constructed, how it was used, and where the effects of aging and wear should be.

One way to ensure authenticity is to obtain written documentation, including the guarantee of a cash refund if an object turns out not to be as described on the bill of sale. This method is usually available only if purchasing through a reputable dealer. Auction houses specifically warn prospective buyers to inspect an object before bidding. Property is sold "as is," without any representation or warranty as to correctness of the catalogue description regarding physical condition, size, quality, rarity, importance, medium, or provenance.

Cultural Artifacts

Collectors interested in the historical attributions of many folk art objects aim to include ephemera and other period artifacts in their collections. Indian club memorabilia is no exception. Championship medals, ribbons, and trophies were awarded to athletes who excelled in Indian-

club exercises. Advertisements, catalogues, and manuals illustrating typical exercises can be found dating back to the 1860s. Salesmen's samples included full size but hollow clubs, as well as miniatures (page 51). Other collectibles include jewelry, trade cards, posters, lithographs, certificates, and photographs. Such items are treasured finds.

Above: Silver-plated Elgin pocket watch engraved with initials "MB," dated "Dec. 25, 1894," with a decorative fob featuring two miniature Indian clubs. Quite a gift for an Indian club devotee!

Clockwise, from top left:

This ribbon of excellence was awarded at an Indian-club competition held at a "Turnverein," in Holyoke, Massachusetts. Turnvereins were gymnastic institutions established by German immigrants. Members of these institutions were called "Turners." They were known for their commitment to physical fitness.

A silver-plated cup made by N. G. Wood & Sons of Boston features the insignia for "M.I.T.A.C.," an athletic association established in 1879. The insignia bears an Indian club with two crossed swords. The cup is inscribed "Second Prize Running High Jump Mar. 14, 1896 E. H. Clark."

Commemorative medals were often awarded at Indian club competitions. The smaller of the two medals shown here is a bar pin with a hanging disk. The initials "F. L." are engraved in the cross bar. The disk features a design of crossed Indian clubs and two dumbbells. The larger medal, a gold-plated coin with a raised design, depicts three gymnasts, one holding a pair of Indian clubs while the other two look on. An array of exercise equipment is featured in the background.

A silver-plated "loving cup," made by Wallace Bros., is engraved with the initials of an athletic institution, "AAC," on each of its three sides. A name and date are inscribed on each side as well. The side of the trophy featuring Clinton DeWitt, the Indian club exercise winner of 1912, is shown here. The other two sides are inscribed with the name of John Cole, who won the competition in 1913 and again in 1914.

Above: Artist unknown. *Buttons*. c. 1860s–1930s. Wood with applied buttons, H 27 x Diam. 4½″, Weight 6½ lbs. Private collection

The artist who created this button-encrusted club, one of a pair, was so precise in the placement of every button that the clubs mirror each other. There are over three hundred period buttons on each club.

Opposite: Artist unknown. *Indian Clubs*. c. 1860s–1930s. Inlaid white and black walnut. Private collection

Inlaid Indian clubs were made of white and black walnut and varied in size, shape, and in the geometry of their inlaid patterns. Note the similarity of design between the salesman's sample and the full-size clubs.

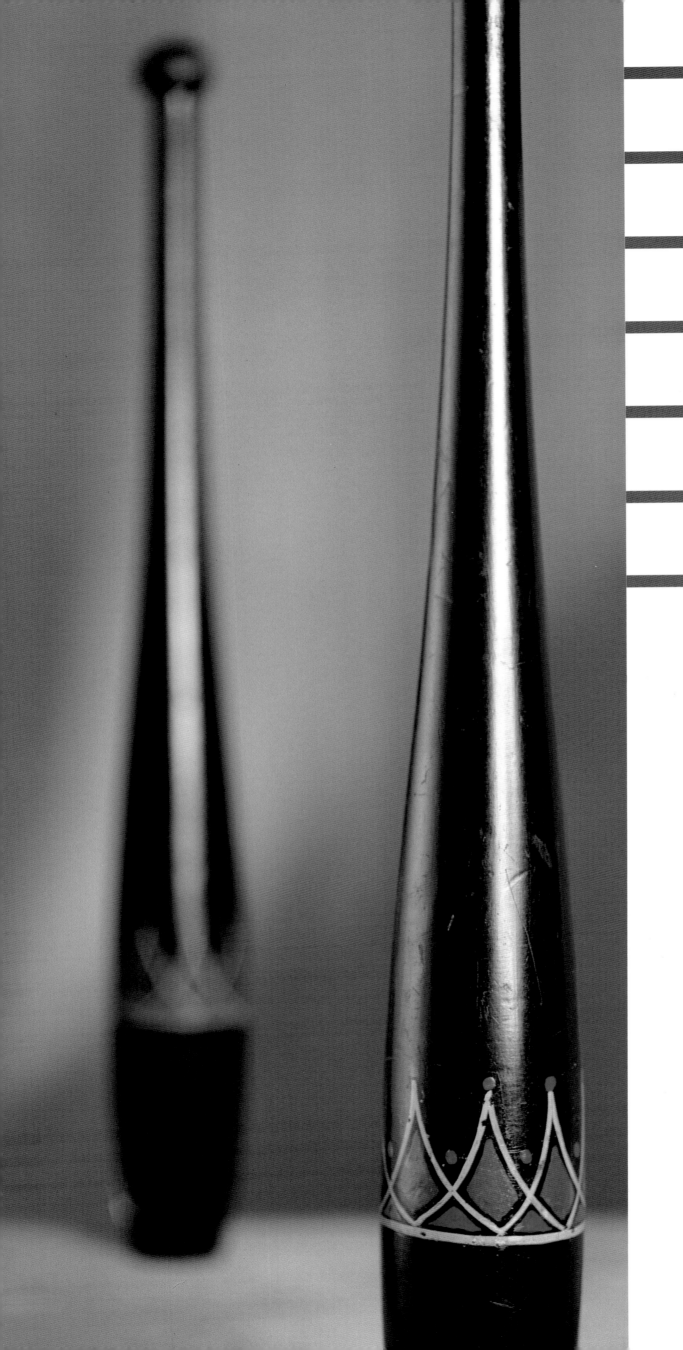

Left: Artist unknown. *Indian Clubs.*
c. 1860s–1930s. Polychromed wood,
H 20 x Diam. 2″, Weight ½ lb.
Private collection

These painted clubs are unusual for their
length, twenty inches, in relation to
their weight, one-half pound. They were
either demonstration clubs or ladies' clubs.
Lightweight children's clubs would not
have been this long.

Opposite: Artist Unknown. *All Flags Flying.*
c. 1876. Polychromed wood, H 25 x Diam. 5″,
Weight 6 lbs. Collection of Michael and
Marilyn Gould

The American Flag has long been a popular
folk art motif. This was particularly true
around the time of the nation's centennial.

Above: Artist unknown. *Indian Clubs in Custom Carrying Case*. c. 1860s–1930s.
Inlaid black and white walnut, H 21 x Diam. 5½″, Weight 5 lbs. Private collection

This pair of stylized, inlaid black and white walnut clubs with its own customized carrying case
is a testament to the maker's craftsmanship and artistic ability. The trumpet-turned side
supports and inlaid geometric pattern of the case complement the shape and inlaid pattern of
the clubs. The base of the case features two holders in which the clubs rest. The top of the case
has two openings through which the club handles are stabilized. The elaborate nature of this set
suggests that it was specially designed for a serious Indian club swinger.

Right: Artists unknown. *"Short" Club and Salesmen's Samples.* c. 1860s–1930s. Full-size club, inlaid black and white walnut, H 14 x Diam. 3″, Weight 1½ lbs.; samples, metal and wood, H 3–5″. Private collection

A "short" full-size Indian club towers over a progression of salesmen's samples. The samples were made of the same variety of woods, in similar shape and proportion, and with the same surface treatments as standard-size clubs. Samples were also made of metal, although no full-size Indian club has been found in this material.

Below: This "stadium" of Indian clubs was featured in Bert Savage's booth at the Manchester, New Hampshire, Antiques Dealers Association Show. The combination of decorative and plain wood clubs makes for an arresting display.

The Collector

Having attempted to establish guidelines for collecting Indian clubs there remains one key intangible, a driving force behind any collection—you, the collector. As articulated by historian Kenneth L. Ames:

> A collection cannot be fully understood without knowing something about its collectors. Collections are usually deeply revealing about the people who create them. Collections record or objectify personal journeys or sagas; they are the tangible expressions of intellectual, emotional, or spiritual growth and development.[23]

Ask a group of collectors what is beautiful, and the answers will be myriad. As has so often been said, "beauty is in the eyes of the beholder." Therefore, the final question to be answered when considering whether or not to add an object to your collection is, "Do you love it?" If it appeals to you aesthetically, if you sense its rhythm and balance, if it has visual impact—and the price is right—add that Indian club to your collection.

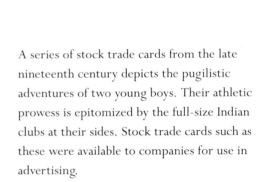

A series of stock trade cards from the late nineteenth century depicts the pugilistic adventures of two young boys. Their athletic prowess is epitomized by the full-size Indian clubs at their sides. Stock trade cards such as these were available to companies for use in advertising.

Below: *College-Graduating Days Have Come!* Original chromolithograph, published by Sackett & Wilhelms, New York, late nineteenth century. Each graduate is "armed for the fight of life." Harvard and Yale men proudly display their accomplishments with athletic equipment, including oversized Indian clubs, while the Vassar graduate leaves with her textbooks on "How to be Beautiful," "Rules of Tennis," "Art of Flirtation," "Fashion Bazaar," and "How to Dance."

Chapter Three
PERSONAL REFLECTIONS

*A collection that only provides visual delight has value, but
that value is modest compared to a collection that sets people off on
explorations of their own.*

—*Kenneth L. Ames*[1]

Collecting is a passion. An obsession. The rush of adrenaline as
the gate to the flea market or the door to the antique show
opens. The thrill of "the find." A full range of emotions is felt
each time the hunt begins for that ever-elusive object. Oh, the joy of
adding to your collection and the despair of reaching a booth one step
behind another collector—seeing a sold sign or red dot on an object
that was "almost" yours. Yet, optimism abounds; there is always the
hope of finding an even better example of the "one that got away"
down the next aisle or at next month's show. Collecting is a "field of
dreams"—an addiction of highs and lows most collectors would never
choose to give up. A commentary on the state of collecting among
Americans in the Sept. 22, 1929, edition of the New York *Herald
Tribune* is as timely today as then:

> America today is a nation of collectors more cosmopolitan
> than any the world has ever known. Yet in the midst of
> cosmopolitanism our collectors remain finely national. The
> most widespread love among them is for the relics of our
> ancestors. The majority of our collectors want to surround
> themselves—especially in their country houses, where they
> have the most leisure—with the furniture of our forebears,
> the portraits of our early Americans and the china, glass and
> precious bric-a-brac of those who gave our nation to us. This
> Americana passion is so widespread at present as to be an
> epidemic rage.[2]

Above right: A sign, "Welcome, Church Entrance," points the way
to a guest room. Indian clubs and a "Mogul" windmill weight are
displayed in specially designed nooks outside the room.

Right: A living-room window provides a perfect setting for pairs of
Indian clubs. Wooden hearse curtains from the late eighteenth century
furnish just the right amount of privacy. A basket of clubs sits on the
floor next to a New Jersey grain-painted nineteenth-century chest that
acts as a pedestal for folk art sculptures and a pair of "large" clubs. At
one time, these clubs, twenty-eight inches in length and weighing fifteen pounds each, were embellished with tin stars. Today, one star and
the tacks that held the others are the only vestiges remaining, a testament to what was once a truly spectacular pair of clubs.

Above: Architectural tie-rod bolt plates in a multitude of sizes and colors cover a bedroom wall, creating a "shower" of stars to wish upon each night. They provide a striking background for a collection of Indian clubs. A pair of clubs from England have been included in this display. Their rounded bases render them unable to stand on their own.

Inset: Sunlight is reflected in a New Jersey fanlight that spans the back wall of a bedroom. Three sets of decorated Indian clubs sit on top of a "Newton & Kingsley" cupboard. The two iron beds, one white and one green in their "found" condition, were bought from Hob Nail, a great place to find iron and brass beds in New York State.

Above: A colorful assortment of Indian clubs complements an early-
nineteenth-century folk art painting, *Generations*, depicting a grandmother,
daughter, and son. The clubs and the painting have something in common—
they are the work of anonymous artists.

Our Story

A collection is a biography without words, in which individual objects may be places visited, significant experiences or personal epiphanies.

—*Michael D. Hall*[3]

My husband and I attended our first antique show in 1970, the first year we were married. We were fortunate to be in the company of a couple who had been collecting American folk art for over twenty years. They encouraged and helped educate us in our pursuit and knowledge of folk art. Yet, they were not solely academic mentors. They inspired us to rely on our "gut" reaction, particularly on aesthetic issues. If an object doesn't speak to us on an emotional and aesthetic level or doesn't increase our knowledge of history, we don't add it to our collection.

We began collecting Indian clubs by chance. A journey through Pennsylvania in 1982 led us to Marietta, a quaint town lined with antique shops. At The Secret Cupboard, Ronald spotted four objects that appeared to us to be jugglers' pins painted red and blue with white stars. We were immediately drawn to their sculptural impact as they stood lined up together in patriotic splendor. The dealer explained to us that these were not jugglers' pins but Indian clubs, exercise equipment popular in America during the late nineteenth century, and that the patriotic design was inspired by the 1876 celebration of the American centennial. We had never seen or heard of Indian clubs but knew we couldn't leave the shop without them. We were hooked. Today, we own over three hundred Indian clubs.

Clubs have great appeal in numbers. As Roger Rose, a friend and fellow collector-competitor, describes them, in groups the clubs are "almost like a perennial garden."

As our collection began to grow, so too did our determination to learn more about the subject. We began to seek information and cultural artifacts that would help us understand the historical perspective of Indian clubs. We acquired manuals, trade cards, photographs, trophies, and jewelry. With this book we share our knowledge of Indian clubs.

The chronicle of our collection happily still continues, for the joys of collecting never end.

—*Nina Fletcher Little*[4]

Above left: Artist unknown. *1876 Centennial Foursome.* c. 1876. Polychromed wood, H 18 x Diam. 3″, Weight 1½ lbs.; H 15½ x Diam. 2½″, Weight ¾ lb. Private collection

America celebrated its 100th year of independence in 1876. This decorative foursome, in red and blue with white stars and black stripes, might have been proudly swung as a testament to patriotism.

Above right: Alice and Ronald Hoffman surrounded by folk art sculptures— a swan, a mermaid, and a wheel of fortune. All were created by Ronald. A pair of Indian clubs sporting "Naughty Nellies" is among the collection of clubs in the foreground. The table on the right with its apron of hearts was designed and grain-painted by Alice.

NOTES

Introduction

1. Numerous publications have addressed these varied perspectives. On art of the common man, see: Holger Cahill, *American Folk Sculpture: The Work of Eighteenth and Nineteenth-Century Craftsmen* (Newark, 1931), 13–8; Cahill, *American Folk Art: The Art of the Common Man in America 1750–1900* (New York, 1932), 6–28; Beatrice T. Rumford, "Uncommon Art of the Common People: A Review of Trends in the Collecting and Exhibiting of American Folk Art" in Ian M. G. Quimby and Scott T. Swank, eds., *Perspectives in American Folk Art* (New York, 1980), 13–53. On community context, see: John Michael Vlach and Simon J. Bronner, eds. "Introduction to the New Edition," in *Folk Art and Art Worlds* (Logan, Utah, 1992), xv–xxi. Includes bibliography of publications since 1980. On folk art as social history, see: Michael D. Hall, "Through a Collector's Eye: A Changing View of American Folk Sculpture," in *Stereoscopic Perspective: Reflections on American Fine and Folk Art* (Ann Arbor, Mich., 1988), 125–40; Scott Graham Williamson, *The American Craftsman* (New York, 1940), 1–12. On personal expression, see: Herbert W. Hemphill, Jr., ed., *Folk Sculpture USA* (Brooklyn, 1976), 7–8; Maurice Tuchman, Carol S. Eliel, et al., *Parallel Visions: Modern Artists and Outsider Art* (Los Angeles and Princeton, 1992). See also Alice Winchester's comments regarding the term folk art in "Introduction" to *The Flowering of American Folk Art*. Winchester states that "discussions of terminology for the whole field can go on endlessly, and they have." (New York, 1974), 9; Jack T. Ericson, ed., "What is American Folk Art? A Symposium," in *Folk Art in America* (New York, 1979), 14–21. Thirteen specialists were asked "What is American folk art?" Each had a differing view and definition of folk art.

2. Further discussion regarding changes occurring within the field of folk art can be found in Russell Bowman, "Introduction," *Common Ground/Uncommon Vision: The Michael and Julie Hall Collection of American Folk Art* (Milwaukee, 1993), 13–21; Lynda Roscoe Hartigan, *Made with Passion: The Hemphill Folk Art Collection* (Washington, D.C., 1990).

3. See Hall, 125–40; Jean Lipman, Robert Bishop, Elizabeth V. Warren, and Sharon L. Eisenstat, *Five Star Folk Art: One Hundred American Masterpieces* (New York, 1990); Elizabeth V. Warren and Stacy C. Hollander, *Expressions of a New Spirit: Highlights from the Permanent Collection of the Museum of American Folk Art* (New York, 1989), 8–15. See also Nina Fletcher Little's commentary "What is American Folk Art? A Symposium," in Ericson, ed., *Folk Art in America*, 19.

4. Cahill, *American Folk Sculpture*, 13; and Cahill, *American Folk Art*, 19–28.

5. Robert Bishop, *Folk Painters of America* (New York; 1979), 57–9, 91–2, 104–5; Jean Lipman and Alice Winchester, *The Flowering of American Folk Art: 1776–1876* (New York, 1974), 15–63.

6. Harvey Green, *Fit For America: Health, Fitness, Sport and American Society* (Baltimore, 1986), 181–215; Sim. D. Kehoe, *The Indian Club Exercise with Explanatory Figures and Positions* (New York, 1866), 17–26.

Chapter One

1. Williamson, 7.

2. N. L. Nigam, Director of Salarjung Museum, Hyderabad, India, to Alice J. Hoffman, Nov. 18, 1990. Correspondence regarding origin of the Indian club. During the Gupta Age in North India, the battle club, representing one of Lord Vishnu's attributes, was further deified as a goddess and named Gada Devi. Subsequently, as a representation of the Gada's personified form, Vishnu is seen holding the Gada Devi in one of his lower hands. During the Islamic period the battle club was also known as Gurz. The form of the club changed dramatically during the medieval period. The head was provided with metal spikes, making it more deadly. Other names that represent the various forms of the club, such as Musaa and Mugda, can be found in Sanskrit literature.

3. Kehoe, 8.

4. Ibid.

5. Robert Bishop and Patricia Coblentz, *The World of Antiques, Art, and Architecture in Victorian America* (New York, 1979), 11.

6. Kehoe, 8.

7. Ibid., 9.

8. Green, 182.

9. Ibid., 184.

10. Kehoe, 8.

11. J. H. Dougherty, *Indian Clubs and Dumb Bells* (New York, 1892), 7.

12. Ibid., 172.

13. Dio Lewis, A.M., M.D., *The New Gymnastics for Men, Women and Children* (New York, 1888), 19.

14. Benjamin Gardiner, *Indian Club Swinging by an Amateur* (Providence, 1884), 5.

15. M. Bornstein, *Manual of Instruction in the Use of Dumb Bell, Indian Club and Other Athletic Exercises* (New York, 1889), 7.

16. Ibid., 14–5.

17. Gardiner, 9.

18. Ibid.

19. W. G. Anderson, "Introduction," in *Club Swinging for Physical Exercise and Recreation* (Boston, 1908), 9–10.

20. J. Madison Watson, *Hand-Book of Calisthenics and Gymnastics: A Complete Drill-Book for Schools, Families, and Gymnasiums with Music to Accompany the Exercises* (New York and Philadelphia, 1864), 250, 384.

21. Kehoe, 22.

22. Dougherty, 7.

23. Norman Anthony, ed., "Indian Club Mania Grows," *BallyHoo* 4, no. 1 (Feb. 1933): 23.

24. Shirley M. Stadnick, Manager Consumer Relations, Spalding Sports Worldwide, Chicopee, Massachusetts, to Alice J. Hoffman, Dec. 3, 1985. Correspondence regarding the production and manufacture of Indian clubs.

Chapter Two

1. Robert Bishop, Judith Reiter Weissman, Michael McManus, and Henry Niemann, *Folk Art: Paintings, Sculpture & Country Objects* (New York, 1983), 19.

2. Gerard C. Wertkin, Director of Museum of American Folk Art, to Alice J. Hoffman, Dec. 1994, June 1995. Conversations regarding Shaker community.

3. Watson, 259.

4. Ibid., 260.

5. Kehoe, 79.

6. Ibid., 29–30.

7. Watson, 260.

8. Kehoe, 25, notes that "at [an] exhibition [at the Olympic Club in San Francisco], Mr. Charles Bennett, who is termed the 'young California Hercules,' used twenty-pound Clubs in a variety of movements, and held fifty-two pounds in each hand, at arm's length, with ease."

9. Ibid., 23–5.

10. Ibid., 71.

11. *The Gymnasium* 6, no. 2 (Mar.–Apr. 1895): 9.

12. Ibid.

13. Ibid.

14. G. T. B. Cobbett and A. F. Jenkin, "Introduction," *Indian Clubs: The All-England Series* (London, c. 1900), 2.

15. Dougherty, 7.

16. Sotheby's, *The American Folk Art Collection of Howard and Catherine Feldman* (5744 "Feldman," New York, June 23, 1988), Lot no. 132.

17. Sotheby's, *American Folk Art from the Collection of Mr. and Mrs. G. William Holland of Pennsylvania* (6659 "Holland," New York, Jan. 28, 1995), Lot. no. 661.

18. Herman Weiskopf, *The Perfect Game* (New York, 1978), and Edward F. Dolan, Jr., *The Complete Beginner's Guide to Bowling* (New York, 1974).

19. Peck & Snyder, *Price List of Out & Indoor Sports & Pastimes* (New York, c. 1900).

20. Kit Summers, *Juggling with Finesse: The Definitive Book of Juggling* (San Diego, 1987), 180.

21. Frank E. Miller, *Indian Club Swinging: One, Two and Three Club Juggling* (New York, Akron, and Chicago, 1900), 136–82.

22. For an interesting discussion see Samuel Pennington, *April Fool: Folk Art Fakes and Forgeries, the Catalogue of an Exhibition at Hirschl & Adler Folk Presented by the Museum of American Folk Art* (Waldoboro, Me., 1988).

23. Kenneth L. Ames, "Folk Art and Cultural Values," in *Common Ground/Uncommon Vision*, 83.

Chapter Three

1. Ames, in *Common Ground/Uncommon Vision*, 83.

2. Quoted in Wendy A. Cooper, "Introduction," *In Praise of America: American Decorative Arts 1650–1830* (New York, 1980), 40.

3. Hall, 138.

4. Nina Fletcher Little, *Little by Little: Six Decades of Collecting American Decorative Arts* (New York, 1984), 278.

BIBLIOGRAPHY

Ames, Kenneth. *Beyond Necessity: Art in the Folk Tradition.* Winterthur, Del.: Henry Francis du Pont Winterthur Museum, 1977.

Anderson, W. G., M.D., Professor of Physical Education. "Introduction," in *Club Swinging for Physical Exercise and Recreation.* Boston: n.p., 1908.

Anthony, Norman, ed. "Indian Club Mania Grows." *BallyHoo* 4, no. 1 (Feb. 1933): 23.

Armstrong, Tom, et al. *Two Hundred Years of American Sculpture.* New York: David R. Godine, Publisher, in association with the Whitney Museum of American Art, 1976.

Benedict, George H. *Wright & Ditson's Complete Manual of Boxing, Club-Swinging & Dumb Bell Exercise.* Boston: Wright & Ditson, c. 1880s.

Bishop, Robert. *American Folk Sculpture.* New York: E. P. Dutton, 1974.

_____. *Folk Painters of America.* New York: E. P. Dutton, 1979.

Bishop, Robert, and Patricia Coblentz. *The World of Antiques, Art, and Architecture in Victorian America.* New York: E. P. Dutton, 1979.

Bishop, Robert, Judith Reiter Weissman, Michael McManus, and Henry Niemann. *Folk Art: Paintings, Sculpture & Country Objects.* New York: Alfred A. Knopf, 1983.

Bornstein, M. *Manual of Instruction in the Use of Dumb Bell, Indian Club, and Other Athletic Exercises.* New York: Excelsior Publishing House, 1889.

Burrows, Tom. *The Text-Book of Club-Swinging.* London: Health & Strength, Limited, 1910.

Cahill, Holger. *American Primitives: An Exhibit of the Paintings of Nineteenth-Century Folk Artists.* Newark, N.J.: Newark Museum, 1930.

_____. *American Folk Sculpture: The Work of Eighteenth- and Nineteenth-Century Craftsmen.* Newark, N.J.: Newark Museum, 1931.

_____. *American Folk Art: The Art of the Common Man in America, 1750–1900.* New York: Museum of Modern Art, 1932.

_____. "What is American Folk Art?" *The Magazine Antiques* 58, no. 5 (May 1950): 355–62.

Cobbett, G. T. B., and A. F. Jenkin. *Indian Clubs: The All-England Series.* London, c. 1900.

Common Ground/Uncommon Vision: The Michael and Julie Hall Collection of American Folk Art in the Milwaukee Art Museum. Essays by Lucy R. Lippard, Jeffrey R. Hayes, Kenneth L. Ames; Introduction and interview by Russell Bowman. Milwaukee: Milwaukee Art Museum, 1993.

Cooper, Wendy A. "Introduction." *In Praise of America: American Decorative Arts 1650–1830.* New York: Alfred A. Knopf, 1980.

Dolan, Edward F., Jr. *The Complete Beginner's Guide to Bowling.* New York: Doubleday & Co., 1974.

Dougherty, J. H. *Indian Clubs and Dumb Bells.* Spalding's Athletic Library, vol. 1, no. 2. New York: American Sports Publishing Co., 1892.

Drepperd, Carl W. *America Pioneer Arts and Artists.* Springfield, Mass.: Pond-Ekberg Co., 1942.

Ericson, Jack T., ed. *Folk Art in America: Painting and Sculpture.* New York: The Main Street Press and Mayflower Books, Inc., 1979.

Fales, Dean A., Jr. *American Painted Furniture 1660–1880.* New York: E. P. Dutton, 1979.

Gardiner, Benjamin. *Indian Club Swinging by an Amateur.* Providence, R.I.: E. L. Freeman & Co., 1884.

Gilliatt, Mary, and Elizabeth Wilhide. *Period Style.* Boston: Little, Brown and Co., 1990.

Green, Harvey. *Fit For America: Health, Fitness, Sport and American Society.* Baltimore: The John Hopkins University Press, 1986.

Green, Harvey, and Mary-Ellen Perry. *The Light of the Home: An Intimate View of the Lives of Women in Victorian America.* New York: Pantheon Books, 1983.

The Gymnasium. Ed. Ellen LeGarde. The Narragansett Machine Co., vol. 6, nos. 2, 5, 6 (Mar.–Apr., Sept.– Oct., Nov.–Dec. 1895); vol. 7, nos. 1, 4, 5 (Jan.–Feb., July–Aug., Sept.–Oct., 1896).

Hall, Michael D. *Stereoscopic Perspective: Reflections on American Fine and Folk Art.* Ann Arbor, Mich.: UMI Research Press, 1988.

Hartigan, Lynda Roscoe. *Made with Passion: The Hemphill Folk Art Collection.* Washington, D.C.: Smithsonian Institution Press, 1990.

Hemphill, Herbert W., Jr., ed. *Folk Sculpture USA.* Brooklyn: The Brooklyn Museum, 1976.

Hemphill, Herbert W., Jr., and Julia Weissman. *Twentieth-Century Folk Art and Artists.* New York: E. P. Dutton, 1974.

Jones, Michael Owen. *Exploring Folk Art: Twenty Years of Thought on Craft, Work, and Aesthetics.* Ann Arbor, Mich.: UMI Research Press, 1987.

Kehoe, Sim. D. *The Indian Club Exercise with Explanatory Figures and Positions.* New York: Peck & Snyder, 1866.

Leopold, Allison Kyle. *Living with and Collecting Victoriana.* New York: Clarkson Potter, 1991.

Lewis, Dio, A.M., M.D. *The New Gymnastics for Men, Women and Children.* 24th ed. New York: The Canfield Publishing Company, 1888.

Lipman, Jean. *American Folk Art in Wood, Metal and Stone.* New York: Pantheon Books, 1948.

Lipman, Jean, and Alice Winchester. *The Flowering of American Folk Art: 1776–1876.* New York: The Viking Press, in cooperation with the Whitney Museum of American Art, 1974.

Lipman, Jean, Robert Bishop, Elizabeth V. Warren, and Sharon L. Eisenstat. *Five Star Folk Art: One Hundred American Masterpieces.* New York: Harry N. Abrams, Inc., in association with the Museum of American Folk Art, 1990.

Little, Nina Fletcher. *Little by Little: Six Decades of Collecting American Decorative Arts.* New York: E. P. Dutton and Co., Inc., 1984.

Meyer, George H. *American Folk Art Canes: Personal Sculpture.* Detroit: Sandringham Press, 1992.

Miele, Frank J., ed. "Folk or Art? A Symposium." *The Magazine Antiques* 135, no. I (Jan. 1989): 272–87.

Miller, Frank E. *Indian Club Swinging: One, Two and Three Club Juggling.* New York, Akron, and Chicago: The Saalfield Publishing Co., 1900.

Nigam, N. L., Director of Salarjung Museum, Hyderabad, India, to Alice J. Hoffman, Nov. 18, 1990. Correspondence regarding the origin of Indian clubs.

Partridge Co., Horace. *Illustrated Catalogue of Fall and Winter Sports Gymnasium Goods, Etc.* Boston: The Horace Partridge Co., 1896–97.

Peck & Snyder. *Price List of Out & Indoor Sports & Pastimes.* New York: Peck & Snyder, c. 1900.

Pennington, Samuel. *April Fool: Folk Art Fakes and Forgeries, the Catalogue of an Exhibition at Hirschl & Adler Folk Presented by the Museum of American Folk Art.* Waldoboro, Me.: Maine Antiques Digest, 1988.

Playground and Recreation Association of America. *Athletic Badge Tests for Boys and Girls.* Washington, D.C.: United States Government Printing, 1927.

Quimby, Ian M. G., and Scott T. Swank, eds. *Perspectives in American Folk Art.* New York: W. W. Norton and Co., 1980.

Ricco, Roger, and Frank Maresca, with Julia Weissman. *American Primitive: Discoveries in Folk Sculpture.* New York: Alfred A. Knopf, 1988.

Schatz, W. J. *Club Swinging for Physical Exercise and Recreation.* Boston: American Gymnasia Company, 1908.

Simpson, Milton. *Folk Erotica: Celebrating Centuries of Erotic Americana.* New York: HarperCollins, 1994.

Sotheby's. *The American Folk Art Collection of Howard and Catherine Feldman.* 5744 "Feldman." New York: Sotheby's, June 23, 1988.

————. *American Folk Art From the Collection of Mr. and Mrs. G. William Holland of Pennsylvania.* 6659 "Holland." New York: Sotheby's, Jan. 28, 1995.

Stadnick, Shirley M., Manager Consumer Relations, Spalding Sports Worldwide, Chicopee, Massachusetts. Letter dated Dec. 3, 1985.

Summers, Kit. *Juggling with Finesse: The Definitive Book of Juggling.* San Diego: Finesse Press, 1987.

Tuchman, Maurice, Carol S. Eliel, et al. *Parallel Visions: Modern Artists and Outsider Art.* Los Angeles and Princeton, N.J.: Los Angeles County Museum of Art and Princeton University Press, 1992.

Vlach, John Michael, and Simon J. Bronner, eds. *Folk Art and Art Worlds.* Ann Arbor, Mich.: UMI Research Press, 1986; 2d ed. Logan: Utah State University Press, 1992.

Warmen, Edward B. *Indian Club Exercises.* Spalding's Athletic Library, vol. 14, no. 166. New York: American Sports Publishing Co., 1899.

Warren, Elizabeth V., and Stacy C. Hollander. *Expressions of a New Spirit: Highlights from the Permanent Collection of the Museum of American Folk Art.* New York: Museum of American Folk Art, 1989.

Watson, J. Madison. *Hand-Book of Calisthenics and Gymnastics: A Complete Drill-Book for Schools, Families, and Gymnasiums, with Music to Accompany the Exercises.* New York and Philadelphia: Schermerhorn Bancroft & Co., 1864.

Wegener, Albert B. *Graded Calisthenics and Dumb Bell Drills.* Spalding's Athletic Library, vol. 15, no. 214. New York: American Sports Publishing Co., 1904.

Weiskopf, Herman. *The Perfect Game.* New York: Rutledge Books, Inc., 1978.

Wheelwright, Samuel T. *A New System of Instruction in the Indian Club Exercises; Containing a Simple and Accurate Explanation of all the Graceful Motions as Practised by Gymnasts, Pugilists, Etc.* New York: Thomas O'Kane, 1871.

Williamson, Scott Graham. *The American Craftsman.* New York: Crown Publishers, 1940.

RESOURCE DIRECTORY

The following resource directory is divided into categories: Antique show managers and their events, flea markets, antique dealers, and newspapers and directories. This list consists of places where Indian clubs and related material have been "spotted" or purchased. It is by no means inclusive and should not discourage a collector from seeking new sources.

Show Managers and Their Events

The following promoters organize antique shows that attract a diverse group of individual antique dealers. Such shows take place in armories, gymnasiums, and schools, or outdoors under tents. There is an entry fee. Collectors can often gain early admission for a premium. Early admission policy is advertised in advance. Plan ahead. Call or write to find out specifics.

APPLE HILL PROMOTIONS
P.O. Box 4853
Manchester, NH 03108
603/669-2911
RIVERSIDE ANTIQUES SHOW, Manchester, NH (Aug.)

BARN STAR PRODUCTIONS
FRANK GAGLIO
P.O. Box 775
Wurtsboro, NY 12790
914/888-0509
MID-WEEK IN MANCHESTER, Bedford, NH (Aug.)

BRIMFIELD ASSOCIATES
Box 1800
Ocean City, NJ 08226
609/926-1800
ATLANTIQUE CITY, Atlantic City, NJ (Mar. and Sept.)

M. BRUSHER
P.O. Box 1512
Ann Arbor, MI 48106
313/662-9453
ANN ARBOR ANTIQUES MARKET, Ann Arbor, MI (monthly)

JIM BURKE ANTIQUE SHOWS
York Fairgrounds
West Market Street
Route 462 W
York, PA 17404
717/397-7209
YORK ANTIQUE SHOWS, York, PA (May, June/July, Nov. and Dec.)

COASTAL PROMOTIONS, INC.
Union, ME
207/563-1013
MAINE ANTIQUES FESTIVAL AT THE FAIRGROUNDS, Union, ME (Aug.)

CREATIVE MANAGEMENT PRODUCTIONS
Box 343
Holt, MI 48842
517/676-2079
SUPERFEST ANTIQUES & COLLECTORS EVENT, (Mason) Lansing, MI (Oct.)

DE PASQUALE ENTERPRISES
Box 278
Selden, NY 11784
516/696-0278
CLASSIC ANTIQUES MARKET, Southampton, NY (July, Aug., and Sept.)
ANTIQUES & ELEMENTS OF DESIGN, Bridgehampton, NY (Aug.)

FORBES & TURNER ANTIQUES SHOWS
45 Larchwood Road
South Portland, ME 04106
207/767-3967
DORSET ANTIQUES FESTIVAL, Dorset, VT (biannual, July and Sept.)
GLASTONBURY ANTIQUES FESTIVAL, Glastonbury, CT (Aug.)
HILDENE'S ANTIQUES SHOW, Manchester, VT (biannual, July and Sept.)
NATHAN HALE ANTIQUES FESTIVAL, Coventry, CT (July)
REDDING ANTIQUES FAIR, Redding, CT (June)

J & J PROMOTIONS
P.O. Box 385, Route 20
Brimfield, MA 01010
413/245-3436
J & J SHOW, Brimfield, MA (May, July, and Sept.)

STEVE JENKINS
P.O. Box 632
Westfield, IN 46074
317/896-5341
TAILGATE ANTIQUE SHOW, Nashville, TN (Oct. and Jan. or Feb.)

N. PENDERGAST JONES
158 Water Street
Stonington, CT 06378
203/535-1995
CARAMOOR FALL ANTIQUES SHOW, Katonah, NY (Sept.)
NANTUCKET ANTIQUES SHOW, Nantucket, MA (July)

RICHARD E. KRAMER & ASSOCIATES
427 Midvale Avenue
St. Louis, MO 63130
314/862-1091
800/862-1090
HEART OF COUNTRY ANTIQUE SHOW, Nashville, TN (Oct. and Feb.)

MADISON-BOUCKVILLE MGT.
P.O. Box 97
Hamilton, NY 13346
315/824-2462
MADISON BOUCKVILLE ANTIQUES SHOW, Hamilton, NY (Aug.)

MALDEN BRIDGE PRODUCTIONS
Box 425
Westport Point, MA 02791
508/636-3382
COLUMBIA COUNTRY ANTIQUES & ARCHITECTURAL FAIR, Chatham, NY (July)
TIVERTON FOUR CORNERS ANTIQUES SHOW, Tiverton, RI (July and Aug.)
WESTPORT COUNTRY ANTIQUES FESTIVAL, Westport, MA (July)

DAVID M. AND PETER MANCUSO
Box 667
New Hope, PA 18938
215/862-5828
FAR HILLS ANTIQUES SHOW, Far Hills, NJ (June)

THE MAVEN CO.
Box 1538
Waterbury, CT 06721
203/758-3880
EASTERN STATES ANTIQUES COLLECTIBLES SHOW, Springfield, MA (Oct.)
EASTERN STATES EPHEMERA, BOOK, ADVERTISING & POSTCARD SHOW AND SALE, Springfield, MA (Nov.)

RICHARD MAY
Route 20, P.O. Box 416
Brimfield, MA 01010
413/245-9271
MAY'S ANTIQUE MARKET, Brimfield, MA (May, July, and Sept.)

MCG ANTIQUES PROMOTIONS
10 Chicken Street
Wilton, CT 06897
203/762-3525
BERKSHIRE BOTANICAL GARDEN ANTIQUES SHOW, Stockbridge, MA (July)
HANCOCK SHAKER VILLAGE ANTIQUES SHOW, Pittsfield, MA (July)
WILTON D.A.R. ANTIQUES MARKETPLACE, Wilton, CT (Sept.)
WILTON HISTORICAL SOCIETY ANTIQUES SHOW, Wilton, CT (March)
WILTON OUTDOOR ANTIQUES MARKETPLACE, Wilton, CT (June)

McHUGH PRESENTATIONS
Box 517
Wrentham, MA 02903
508/384-3857
JANUARY PIER ANTIQUE SHOW, New York, NY (Jan.)
McHUGH'S PIER EXTRAVAGANZA, New York, NY (Sept.)
SOUTHAMPTON ANTIQUES SHOW, Southampton, NY (Sept.)
THE VINEYARD ANTIQUES SHOW, Edgartown (Martha's Vineyard), MA (July)

METROPOLITAN ART & ANTIQUE SHOWS
110 West 19th Street
New York, NY 10011
212/463-0200
METROPOLITAN ANTIQUARIAN BOOK FAIR, NY (Sept. and Nov.)
METROPOLITAN EPHEMERA FAIR, New York, NY (Sept.)
METROPOLITAN VICTORIANA SHOW, New York, NY (Oct.)

DON AND PAM MORIARTY
Box 26
Brimfield, MA 01010
413/245-9556
BRIMFIELD'S HEART-O-THE-MART, Brimfield, MA (May, July, and Sept.)

THE NEW HAMPSHIRE ANTIQUES DEALERS ASSOCIATION, INC.
603/286-7506
NEW HAMPSHIRE ANTIQUES SHOW, Manchester, NH (Aug.)

OLIVER & GANNON ASSOCIATES
Box 651
Altamont, NY 12009
518/861-5062
ADIRONDACK MUSEUM ANTIQUES SHOW, Blue Mountain Lake, NY (Sept.)
ALBANY INSTITUTE ANTIQUARIAN BOOK & EPHEMERA FAIR, Albany, NY (Nov.)
SUMMER WESTCHESTER ANTIQUARIAN BOOK & EPHEMERA FAIR, Tarrytown, NY (Aug.)

EDWIN T. PALKO
Box 1
Taconic, CT 06079
203/435-2034
ANTIQUES IN A COW PASTURE, Salisbury, CT (Sept.)
HISTORIC RIDGEFIELD OUTDOOR ANTIQUES MARKET, Ridgefield, CT (June)
KENT OUTDOOR ANTIQUES MARKET, South Kent, CT (Aug.)
LITCHFIELD HILLS ANTIQUES SHOW, New Milford, CT (Aug.)

REVIVAL PROMOTIONS, INC.
P.O. Box 388
Grafton, MA 01519
508/839-9735
FARMINGTON ANTIQUES WEEKEND, Farmington, CT (June and Sept.)

JOHN KRYNICK AND FRAN NESTOR
P.O. Box 297
Analomink, PA 18320
717/424-8993
(by appointment)

CHARLES LLOYD
WASHINGTON CROSSING BOOKS
1112 Taylorville Road
Westchester, PA 18977
215/321-9191
(by appointment)

Newspapers and Directories

Antique shows, flea markets, and auctions occur almost every day of the year. Times, dates, addresses, entrance fees, and buyer's premiums change. Consult the following newspapers and directories for listings of shows, auctions, markets, and dealers across the country.

NEWSPAPERS

Antiques & Arts Weekly
Bee Publishing Company
5 Church Hill Road
Newtown, CT 06470
203/426-3141
(weekly)

The Antique Trader Weekly
P.O. Box 1050
Dubuque, IA 52004
800/334-7165
(weekly)

Folk Art, The Magazine of the Museum of American Folk Art
61 West 62nd Street
New York, NY 10023
212/977-7170
(quarterly)

Maine Antiques Digest
P.O. Box 1429
Waldoboro, ME 04572
207/832-4888
(monthly)

New England Antiques Journal
4 Church Street
Ware, MA 01082
800/432-3505
(monthly)

Ohio Antique Review
12 East Stafford Avenue
Worthington, OH 43085
614/885-9757
(monthly)

DIRECTORIES

Clark's Flea Market USA: A National Directory of Flea Markets and Swap Meets
Clark Publications
419 Garson Point Road
Milton, FL 32570
904/623-0794

The Confident Collector: U.S. Flea Market Directory
Avon Books
1350 Avenue of the Americas
New York, NY 10019
212/261-6800

The Official Directory to U.S. Flea Markets
House of Collectibles
201 East 50 Street
New York, NY 10022
212/751-2600

Acknowledgments

To Ronald A. Hoffman, my husband, who cajoled, organized, screamed, and almost always understood my "crazies." Thank you for your unconditional support and guidance, and for believing that I really could do it. Without you, the deadline would have come and gone many times. I know you love me no matter what—although when my papers were flying from one room of our apartment to the next without an end in sight, and take-out food was our only repast, I think you were having second thoughts!

To my in-laws, Bea and Bernard Manischewitz, who generously underwrote the cost of hiring Bill Abranowicz three years before I even had a book contract—and never asked, "How's that book coming?"

To Milt Simpson and his crew at Johnson & Simpson, thank you for designing the presentation boards I submitted to publishers. Without your extraordinary creativity, this book might never have found a home.

To Helen who introduced me to Bill Abranowicz, an exceptional photographer.

To Bill Abranowicz for his ability to translate through his lens my belief that Indian clubs are art objects. For his calm response to my tracking him down in Toronto, two weeks before the manuscript was due, requesting "just seven more photographs." A special thanks to Laura Moss, his assistant, who transported so many clubs back and forth from New York to New Jersey to New York.

To Gavin Ashworth, whose expertise in black-and-white photography enhanced the period photographs, illustrations, catalogues, and manuals. Gavin never said no to my countless calls for "just one more black-and-white" even with only one day to go! Thank you for your good humor and patience.

To Gerard C. Wertkin, Director of the Museum of American Folk Art, who wrote the foreword for this book, shared his expertise on the Shaker community, and opened so many doors of opportunity for me at the museum.

To Sandy MacGregor and Marilyn Abraham, my "in-house" publishing consultants.

To Krissy Olsen and Nancy Krumholtz for support and research. I'll never look at another bowling pin or juggler's pin without thinking of how you came to my rescue.

To Alice Fleming, Howard Fertig, and Ben Apfelbaum for finding ephemera.

To those who responded to my "Help Needed" requests. Especially N. L. Nigam, Director of Salarjung Museum, Hyderabad, India; Michele Newton, Curator, Powers Museum, Carthage, Mo.; Carol Sandler, The Strong Museum, Rochester, N.Y.; Shirley M. Stadnick, Manager Consumer Relations, Spalding Sports Worldwide, Chicopee, Mass.; Mrs. Helen F. Knipp; Dr. Neil Garonzik; and Andrew G. Whiteside.

To my dealer friends, who constantly inquired, "How's the book coming?"—especially George and Judy Jagg, who tirelessly worked to help expand my collection.

To Bert Savage, who always managed to find a pair of clubs I couldn't live without.

To those who opened their collections to this book. Thank you to Alyce and Roger Rose, "antiquing" compatriots and friends extraordinaire. To Roger in particular, whose competitive spirit is second only to my own. Roger, I just got the last of the forty-eight state ashtrays! To Joe and Peggy Seton for letting us come into their fabulous eighteenth-century farmhouse and rearrange a "few" things. To Michael and Marilyn Gould for *All Flags Flying*. To Bill Lohrman and Steve Wagner,

don't forget, I'm first on the list. To Bill Carr and J. Allen Radford, sorry my budget didn't include a trip west of the Mississippi.

To Elizabeth Warren for encouraging me to expand a "class" assignment.

To Paul Gottlieb, who welcomed me into his office knowing I wasn't the other Alice Hoffman. Thank you for sharing my enthusiasm for Indian clubs and the belief that others would find them historically and artistically interesting.

To Elisa Urbanelli, my editor, and designer Carol Robson for making this book a reality. A heartfelt thank you.

To Maryann Warakomski, my licensing associate, who understood without being asked when I needed her support during the two-week period prior to submitting the manuscript. To Ray for spotting the rack of clubs.

To Valerie Longwood. Thanks for figuring out how to format labels.

To Judy Lewis, always by my side on the "early" admissions line, my bridge partner and friend through thick and thin. To Stanley at the auction house. Thanks for buying the "Vega Cal" man or I never would have known you two.

To Alice Nagel, my blood sister, who suffered through college, through law school, and through this!

To Susan Beatus, who was the first friend I made twenty-five years ago when Ronald and I moved to New York. You've seen and heard it all.

To Barri Hammer and Robin Persky, friends to the end. Thanks for "checking-in" and always listening. Yes, the BOO finally got its K.

To David Hammer for making Ronald look calm.

To Marilyn and Ron Caplan, Helen and Neal Dorman, Wendy Friedman, Cathy Glazer, Andrea and Stephen Granet, Les and Ellen Kreisler, Irwin and Diane Levy, Linda and Peter Linchitz, Judy and Jeff Lubinsky, Gael and Michael Mendelsohn, Susan and Chris Newman, Alice and Mel Prager, Sandi Sachs, Steve Semlitz, and Ellen and Michael Starr. Thanks for understanding why telephone calls and weekends at "Camp Hoffman" came to a halt. Yes, my hair was still wet when I handed in the manuscript.

To Belda and Marcel Lindenbaum, Carol and Mel Newman, and Peggy and Billy Rosenblatt, bridge partners. Thanks for understanding why I trumped when we were playing no trump. What's the Jacoby Transfer?

To Ann Hanratty for taking such good care of all my "doo-dads."

To Rachel Weissburg for tolerating the "other" book spread out on the couch for months.

To my mother and sister who adore my "bowling pins."

To Ken and Bette Olsen, my inspiration on every level.

To my many friends, even those who never believed I would finish this book. Your good humor, support, and monthly inquiries, "How's the book coming?" drove me to it! A big grateful hug to all of you—you know who you are.

To Stacey and Jennifer B., Karen and Debbie D., Jason and Lindsay G., Lauren and Ross H., Nevin, Jordan, and Peter K., Rachel-Soleil L., Jonathan and Jordan L., Adam and Lauren L., Adam, Michael, and Jenna P., Gregory and David P., Rachel and Stephen ("Irv") R., Joshua and Rebecca S., Samantha S., and Olivia and Myles S., for sharing so many good times and for letting Ronald and me love you as if you were our own, and to your parents who are such wonderful, generous friends.

To Myles Starr for counting "all" the clubs.

To Adam and Elizabeth, who light up my life. Thanks, Adam, for that special club.

JACQUELINE SIDELI
Box 425
Westport Point, MA
508/636-3382
THE GREENWICH ANTIQUES MARKETS, Old Greenwich,
    CT (Jan., Feb., and Dec.)

SANFORD L. SMITH & ASSOCIATES
68 East Seventh Street
New York, NY 10003
212/777-5218
FALL ANTIQUES SHOW, New York, NY (Sept.–Oct.)
NEW YORK ANTIQUARIAN BOOK FAIR, New York, NY
    (April)
PHILADELPHIA ANTIQUES SHOW, PHILADELPHIA, PA (April)
THE PIER SHOWS, New York, NY (Oct.)

STELLA SHOW MANAGEMENT
163 Terrace Street
Haworth, NJ 07641
201/384-0010
ANTIQUES WEEKEND IN SOMERSET, Somerset, NJ (Aug.)
CAPE MAY ANTIQUES FAIR, Cape May, NJ (July and Aug.)
GREAT AMERICAN COUNTY FAIR, Mahwah, NJ (Sept.)
MANHATTAN ANTIQUES & COLLECTIBLES TRIPLE PIER
    EXPO, New York, NY (two weekends in Nov. and in
    Feb.)
NEW YORK COLISEUM ANTIQUES SHOW, New York, NY
    (Jan., Mar., Oct., and Dec.)
WATERLOO ANTIQUES FAIR, Stanhope, NJ (Sept.)

THE VERMONT ANTIQUES DEALER'S
ASSOCIATION, INC.
802/365-7574
VERMONT ANTIQUES DEALER'S ASSOCIATION ANTIQUE
    SHOW, Bondville, VT (Aug.)

B. WALTER
P.O. Box 310
Red Hook, NY 12571
914/758-6186
RHINEBECK ANTIQUES FAIR, Rhinebeck, NY (May and Sept.)

WENDY ANTIQUES SHOWS
Box 707
Rye, NY 10580
914/698-3442
ARMORY ANTIQUES SHOWS, New York, NY (Feb., Mar.,
    May, and Sept.)
MORRISTOWN ANTIQUES SHOWS, Morristown, NJ (Jan.,
    Mar., Aug., and Nov.)
WHITE PLAINS ANTIQUES SHOWS, White Plains, NY (Jan.,
    April, and Nov.)

Flea Markets

Flea markets occur in the same venue as formal antique
shows. However, there is usually no admission fee. A flea
market offers more of a "junking" experience. Quality
pieces can often be found at bargain prices. Call ahead to
confirm time, place, and dates.

CALIFORNIA

LONG BEACH OUTDOOR ANTIQUES & COLLECTIBLES
MARKET
Veterans Stadium at Lakewood Boulevard
Long Beach, CA 90808
213/655-5703
(third Sunday of every month)

PASADENA CITY COLLEGE FLEA MARKET
Hill Avenue between Colorado and Del Mar
Pasadena, CA 91106
818/585-7906
(first Sunday of every month)

ROSE BOWL FLEA MARKET
Pasadena, CA 91106
213/587-5100
(second Sunday of every month)

CONNECTICUT

ELEPHANT'S TRUNK COUNTRY FLEA MARKET
Route 7
New Milford, CT 06776
203/355-1448
(every Sunday)

MASSACHUSETTS

BRIMFIELD MARKET
P.O. Box 442
Route 20
Brimfield, MA 01010
413/245-9329
(three times a year, May, July, and Sept.)

NEW JERSEY

LAMBERTVILLE ANTIQUES & FLEA MARKET
Route 29, 1½ miles south of Lambertville
Pennington, NJ 08534
609/397-0456
(every Saturday and Sunday)

NEW YORK

STORMVILLE AIRPORT ANTIQUES SHOW & FLEA MARKET
Route 216
Stormville, NY 12583
914/221-6561
(May, July, Aug., and Sept.)

ANNEX ANTIQUES FAIR AND FLEA MARKET
26th Street and Sixth Avenue
New York, NY 10001
212/243-5343
(every Saturday and Sunday)

NORTH CAROLINA

FRANKLIN FLEA AND CRAFT MARKET
199 Highlands Road
Franklin, NC 28734
704/524-6658
(Wednesday, Friday, and Sunday)

JOCKEY LOT ANTIQUES AND FLEA MARKETS
Route 6, Box 206C
Elizabeth City, NC 27909
919/264-3655
(Monday–Saturday)

PENNSYLVANIA

RENNINGER'S ANTIQUE MARKET NO. 1
272 Adamstown
Adamstown, PA 19501
717/385-0104
(every Sunday, plus Antique's & Collector's Extravaganza,
    Apr., June, and Sept.)

RENNINGER'S ANTIQUE MARKET NO. 2
740 Nobel Street
Kutztown, PA
610/683-6848
(every Saturday, plus Antique's & Collector's
    Extravaganza, Apr., June, and Sept.)

Dealers

Many antique dealers have specific areas of interest and
expertise. If you identify a dealer with access to Indian
clubs and related material, that dealer can act as your
"picker." Be sure to inform the dealer of your interest
and economic constraints. In return, the dealer will sup-
ply you with photographs of available items within your

guidelines. Once you establish a rapport with a dealer,
you will have one of the best sources for building your
collection.

Most dealers, even those listed below as owning
shops or available only by appointment, exhibit at
antique shows throughout the year. If you hope to visit
one of the following dealers during your travels, avoid
disappointment—call ahead to confirm store hours or
to make an appointment.

CONNECTICUT

NIKKI AND TOM DEUPREE
480 N. Main Street
Suffield, CT 06078
203/668-7262
(by appointment)

PATTY GAGARIN ANTIQUES
975 Banks North Road
Fairfield, CT 06430
203/259-7332
(by appointment)

PAUL AND MARGARET WELD
P.O. Box 416
Middletown, CT 06457
203/635-3361
(by appointment)

ILLINOIS

HARVEY ANTIQUES
1231 Chicago Avenue
Evanston, IL 60202
708/866-6766
(shop)

FRANK AND BARBARA POLLACK
1214 Green Bay Road
Highland Park, IL 60035
708/433-2213
(by appointment)

IOWA

MAIN STREET ANTIQUES AND ART
Louis Picek
110 West Main
West Branch, IA 52358
319/643-2065
(shop)

MAINE

ROBERTA SACKIN BATT AND MAY DONALDSON
P.O. Box 4150 Sta. A
Portland, ME 04101
207/773-2225
(by appointment)

THE MARSTON HOUSE
Rt. 1, Main Street
Wiscasset, ME 04578
207/882-6010
(shop)

MARYLAND

STELLA RUBIN ANTIQUES
12300 Glen Road
Potomac, MD 20854
301/948-4187
(by appointment)

MASSACHUSETTS

PAM BOYNTON
82 Pleasant Street
Groton, MA 01450
508/448-5031
(by appointment)

ALICE R. FLEMING
EPHEMERA 'N' SORTS
168 North Main Street
Sunderland, MA 01375
413/665-2421
(by appointment)

STEVE FINER
RARE BOOKS
P.O. Box 758
Greenfield, MA 01302
413/773-5811
(by appointment)

FORAGER HOUSE COLLECTION
20 Centre Street
Nantucket, MA 02554
508/228-5977
(shop; *see also* Pennsylvania)

JAGG ANTIQUES
GEORGE AND JUDY JAGG
P.O. Box 69
Holyoke, MA 01041-0069
413/533-7650
(by appointment)

ELAINE RUSH
South Egremont, MA 01258
413/528-8199
(by appointment)

STEPHEN SCORE
73 Chestnut Street
Boston, MA 02108
617/227-9192
(shop)

THE SPLENDID PEASANT
P.O. Box 536
South Egremont, MA 01258
413/528-5755
(shop)

LYNN WEAVER
Essex, MA 01929
617/768-7286
(by appointment)

WENHAM CROSS ANTIQUES
Emily and Irma Lampert
179 Newbury Street
Boston, MA 02116
617/236-0409
(by appointment)

MICHIGAN

ELLIOTT AND ELLIOTT
P.O. Box 751
Harbor Springs, MI 49740
616/526-2040
(by appointment)

HAYMARKET ANTIQUES
60275 Decatur Road
Cassopolis, MI 49031
616/445-2018
(by appointment)

NEW HAMPSHIRE

WILLIAM LEWAN ANTIQUES
Old Troy Road
Fitzwilliam, NH 03447
603/585-3365
(by appointment)

BERT SAVAGE
Larch Lodge
Center Stafford, NH 03815
603/269-7411
(by appointment)

NEW JERSEY

BETTY OSBAND AND PAUL ELLIOTT
R.D. No. 1, Box 293 A
Belvidere, NJ 07823
201/637-6391, 201/628-3697
(by appointment)

NEW MEXICO

ROBERT F. NICHOLS
415 Canyon Road
Santa Fe, NM 87501
505/982-2145
(shop)

NEW YORK

AMERICA HURRAH
766 Madison Avenue
New York, NY 10021
212/535-1930
(shop)

AMERICAN PRIMITIVE GALLERY
594 Broadway, No. 205
New York, NY 10012
212/966-1530
(shop)

MARNA ANDERSON GALLERY
2 Wawarsing Road
New Paltz, NY 12561
914/255-1132
(by appointment)

ARGOSY GALLERY
116 East 59th Street
New York, NY 10022
212/753-4455
(shop)

DENNIS AND VALERIE BAKOLEDIS
109 East Market Street
Rhinebeck, NY 12572
914/876-7944
(by appointment)

BLUE HIGHWAYS ANTIQUES
South Salem, NY 10590
914/533-6326
(by appointment)

DIDI DEGLIN ANTIQUES
Middle Village, NY 11379
718/894-7773
(by appointment)

LAURA FISHER/ANTIQUE QUILTS & AMERICANA
Manhattan Art & Antiques Center
1050 Second Avenue, Gallery No. 84
New York, NY 10022
212/838-2596
(shop)

GAGLIO & MOLNAR
Box 375
Wurtsboro, NY 12790
914/888-5077
(by appointment)

KELTER-MALCE ANTIQUES
74 Jane Street
New York, NY 10014
212/675-7380
(by appointment)

LENNY AND NANCY KISLIN
Bearsville, NY 12409
914/679-8117
(by appointment)

JUDITH AND JAMES MILNE
506 East 74th Street
New York, NY 10021
212/472-0135
(by appointment)

MULESKINNER
10626 Main Street
Clarence, NY 14031
716/759-2261
(shop)

THE OLD PRINT SHOP
150 Lexington Avenue
New York, NY 10016
212/683-3950
(shop)

SUSAN PARRISH
390 Bleecker Street
New York, NY 10014
212/645-5020
(shop)

RICHARD ROMBERG
96 Richmond Street
Rochester, NY 14607
716/546-3785
(by appointment)

PAULA RUBENSTEIN
65 Prince Street
New York, NY 10012
212/966-8954
(shop)

KATHY SCHOEMER AMERICAN ANTIQUES
Box 429
12 McMorrow Lane
North Salem, NY 10560
914/277-8464
(by appointment)

JOHN SIDELI
ARTS & ANTIQUES
Chatham, NY 12037
518/392-2271
(shop)

STUBBS BOOKS & PRINTS
153 East 70th Street
New York, NY 10021
212/772-3120
(shop)

GEORGE WALOWEN AND MICHAEL L. SCHNEIDER
Box 404
Walker Valley, NY 12588
914/744-3916
(by appointment)

BRIAN WINDSOR ART/ANTIQUES
281 Lafayette Street
New York, NY 10012
212/274-0411
(shop)

THOMAS K. WOODARD
799 Madison Avenue
New York, NY 10021
212/988-2906
(shop)

PENNSYLVANIA

FORAGER HOUSE COLLECTION
P.O. Box 82
Washington Crossing, PA 18977
215/493-3007
(shop; *see also* Massachusetts)